IMMORTAL INDIA

Amish is a 1974-born, IIM (Kolkata)-educated banker-turned-author. The success of his debut book, *The Immortals of Meluha* (Book 1 of the Shiva Trilogy), encouraged him to give up his career in financial services to focus on writing. Besides being an author, he is also an Indian-government diplomat, a host for TV documentaries, and a film producer.

Amish is passionate about history, mythology and philosophy, finding beauty and meaning in all world religions. His books have sold more than 7 million copies and have been translated into over 20 languages. His Shiva Trilogy is the fastest-selling and his Ram Chandra Series the second-fastest-selling book series in Indian publishing history. You can connect with Amish here:

- www.facebook.com/authoramish
- www.instagram.com/authoramish
- www.twitter.com/authoramish

Other Titles by Amish

SHIVA TRILOGY

The fastest-selling book series in the history of Indian publishing

The Immortals of Meluha (Book 1 of the Trilogy)

The Secret of the Nagas (Book 2 of the Trilogy)

The Oath of the Vayuputras (Book 3 of the Trilogy)

RAM CHANDRA SERIES

The second-fastest-selling book series in the history of Indian publishing

Ram – Scion of Ikshvaku (Book 1 of the Series)

Sita – Warrior of Mithila (Book 2 of the Series)

Raavan – Enemy of Aryavarta (Book 3 of the Series)

War of Lanka (Book 4 of the Series)

INDIC CHRONICLES

Legend of Suheldev

NON-FICTION

Dharma: Decoding the Epics for a Meaningful Life

Idols: Unearthing the Power of Murti Puja

‘{Amish’s} writings have generated immense curiosity about India’s rich past and culture.’

—Narendra Modi

(Honourable Prime Minister of India)

‘{Amish’s} writing introduces the youth to ancient value systems while pricking and satisfying their curiosity …’

—Sri Sri Ravi Shankar

(Spiritual leader and founder, Art of Living Foundation)

‘{Amish’s writing is} riveting, absorbing and informative.’

—Amitabh Bachchan

(Actor and living legend)

‘Amish is one of India’s greatest storytellers, creative, imaginative, so you have to turn the page.’

—Lord Jeffrey Archer

(One of the highest-selling authors of all time)

‘{Amish’s writing is} a fine blend of history and myth … gripping and unputdownable.’

—BBC

‘Thoughtful and deep, Amish, more than any author, represents the New India.’

—Vir Sanghvi

(Senior journalist and columnist)

‘{Amish} is an extraordinary gift to the world from India. He has done a great service by taking ancient myths and giving them relevance in modern times.’

—Deepak Chopra

(World-renowned spiritual guru and bestselling author)

'{Amish is} one of the most original thinkers of his generation.'

—Arnab Goswami

(Senior journalist and MD, Republic TV)

'Amish has a fine eye for detail and a compelling narrative style.'

—Dr Shashi Tharoor

(Member of Parliament and author)

'{Amish has} a deeply thoughtful mind with an unusual, original and fascinating view of the past.'

—Shekhar Gupta

(Senior journalist and columnist)

'To understand the New India, you need to read Amish.'

—Swapan Dasgupta

(Member of Parliament and senior journalist)

'Through all of Amish's books flows a current of liberal, progressive ideology: about gender, about caste, about discrimination of any kind ... He is the only Indian bestselling writer with true philosophical depth—his books are all backed by tremendous research and deep thought.'

—Sandipan Deb

(Senior journalist and editorial director, Swarajya)

'Amish's influence goes beyond his books, his books go beyond literature, his literature is steeped in philosophy, which is anchored in bhakti, which powers his love for India.'

—Gautam Chikermane

(Senior journalist and author)

'Amish is a literary phenomenon.'

—(Late) Anil Dharker

(Senior journalist and author)

IMMORTAL INDIA

YOUNG COUNTRY, TIMELESS CIVILIZATION

AMISH

HarperCollins *Publishers* India

First published in 2017

This edition published in India by HarperCollins *Publishers* 2024
4th Floor, Tower A, Building No. 10, DLF Cyber City, DLF Phase II,
Gurugram, Haryana – 122002
www.harpercollins.co.in

2 4 6 8 10 9 7 5 3 1

P-ISBN: 978-93-5699-698-4
E-ISBN: 978-93-5699-777-6

Typeset in 11/114 Adobe Garamond Pro at
Manipal Technologies Limited, Manipal

Printed and bound at
Thomson Press (India) Ltd

MIX
Paper | Supporting responsible forestry
FSC® C010615

This book is produced from independently certified FSC® paper
to ensure responsible forest management.

To Bhavna Roy

My sister,
A gyan yogi, a philosopher,
A proud inheritor of Indian wisdom,
A seeker of knowledge from around the world,
One who has often lit my path,
And more importantly, walked with me

Om Namah Shivāya

The universe bows to Lord Shiva.
I bow to Lord Shiva.

Janani Janmabhoomischa Swargadapi Gariyasi

Mother and Motherland are superior to heaven

—Lord Ram, in the Ramayan

Contents

Social Issues

History

Musings

Acknowledgements

The acknowledgements written below were composed when the book was first published in 2017. I must also acknowledge those that are publishing this edition of *Immortal India*. My editor Poulomi; Shabnam and the entire marketing team led by Akriti; Gokul, Vikas, and the entire sales team led by Rahul; the digital marketing team led by Ameya; the Harper360 team Karen, Serena and Darren; all led by Ananth, the brilliant CEO of HarperCollins India, guided by Charlie Redmayne, the CEO of HarperCollins UK, Ireland, India and Australia.

~

This is my first non-fiction book. It is, essentially, a collection of my thoughts on various subjects, crystallized through articles that I wrote, speeches that I made, and debates that I participated in.

There are many who have helped cement, and at times temper, my thoughts. And there are others who have helped bring these thoughts on to public platforms. I'd like to acknowledge some of them.

India, my country, and the land of my karma. I am defined to a great degree by my Indian heritage. My thoughts, my values, my way of life, are moulded by the culture and the heritage of my land.

Neel, my son, my blessing. And in some aspects, my teacher; as I explain in an article in this book.

Preeti, Neel's mother; Bhavna, my sister; Himanshu, my brother-in-law; Anish and Ashish, my brothers; for all their inputs to my articles and speeches. My sister, Bhavna, deserves special mention for the time she invests in reading every article of mine in minute detail, along with her deep advice. My brother-in-law, Himanshu, and my elder brother, Anish, also deserve special mention. Often, they advise me on the broader aspects of the topic, at times tempering my emotional enthusiasm with their sage wisdom.

The rest of my family: Usha, Vinay, Meeta, Donetta, Shernaz, Smita, Anuj, Ruta. For their consistent faith and love.

Gautam, the CEO of Westland, my publisher. A rare combination of efficiency, politeness and old-world manners.

Abhijeet, who has driven the marketing for this book. I have known him for years and he's one of the finest marketing minds I know. It's a delight to receive his support for this book. And Neha, my relationship manager at Westland, who manages all my activities there; multi-talented, enthusiastic, hard-working.

Sudha, my editor. This is the first time I've worked with her. She's a calm, dedicated and meticulous editor. It has been a pleasure and I hope that we get a chance to work together in the future too.

Anuj, my agent. He has been there from the beginning. A constant support and strength.

Some newspapers have been kind enough to give me a regular column (though I am irregular in my writing!), while other media houses have invited me to write one-off articles, some of which have found their way into this book. I'd like to acknowledge them too.

Swagato Ganguly and Neelam Raaj from *The Times of India*, for offering my columns their platform. And more importantly, for their advice, support and patience (especially when, sometimes, months pass by without my writing an article).

Shreevatsa Nevatia and Viju Cherian from the *Hindustan Times*, for the platform, and for the ever supportive and prompt responses.

Suparna Sharma and Amy Fernandes from *The Asian Age/ Deccan Chronicle*, for giving me their platform. They have been friends and early supporters.

Samhita Chakraborty and Sumit Das Gupta from *The Telegraph*, for giving me their platform. And equally importantly, for their advice and feedback.

The Rajasthan Patrika Group of newspapers, for giving me their platform for my Hindi articles.

Phanindra Kumar Devchoudhury of the *Niyomiya Barta*, for giving me a platform for my Assamese articles.

India Today, The Week, Outlook, Good Housekeeping, Femina and 'The Speaking Tree', for giving me their platforms for one-off articles.

Satish, Srivats, Krishnakumar, Deepthi, Sanghamitra, Nidhi, Arunima, Sarita, Amrita, Vipin, Shatrughan, Naveen, Sanyog, Divya, Sateesh, Madhu, Satya Sridhar, Jayasankar and the fantastic team at Westland, my publishers. They have been partners on all my books.

My friend Sagar Pusalkar, Joel D'Leema, Amit Rajbhar, and the entire Quotient team, who, along with the photographer Vaibhav Shedge, created the cover, which looks stunning, despite being burdened with a rather ordinary model!

Hemal, Neha, Hitesh, Natashaa, Candida and the Oktobuzz team, the social media agency for the book. Hardworking, super smart and intensely committed. They are an asset to any team.

Mayank, Vishaal, Priyanka Jain, Deepika, Naresh, Danish, Shreyaa, Abhishek and the Moe's Art team, who have driven communication strategies and marketing alliances for the book. They have been strong partners and among the best agencies I have worked with.

Mohan and Mehul, my managers, who handle almost everything with quiet efficiency, leaving me time to write. Mohan manages all my communication, speeches and media interactions, and Mehul manages the office and accounts.

And last, but certainly not the least, you, the reader. Thank you for all the support you have given to my fiction books. I am now inflicting my first non-fiction book upon you! I hope to receive your continued support and love.

Introduction

Allama Iqbal had character flaws and made errors of judgement. Not least of which was his sectarian espousal of Pakistan, which played a role in poisoning communal relations in pre-Independence India. But that does not take away from the fact that he was a sublime poet. And among his more brilliant lines were these:

> *Yunan-o-Misr-o-Roma sab mit gaye jahan se*
> *Ab tak magar hai baki naam-o-nishan hamara,*
> *Kuchh baat hai ke hasti mit'ti nahin hamari,*
> *Sadiyon raha hai dushman daur-e-zaman hamara.*

> Greek, Egyptians and Romans have all vanished from this world,
> But we are still here,
> There must be something special in us
> That we have not been erased from existence,
> Despite the revolution of time having been our enemy for centuries (that is, despite the tide of history being against us for centuries).

Iqbal was right. The ancient Greek, Egyptian and Roman cultures are museum pieces today, their knowledge and philosophies appropriated by a Judeo-Christian Western world. The ancient cultures of the Central, South and North Americans, Celts, Nordics, Mesopotamians and many others are largely extinct. But ancient Indian culture, despite repeated massive attacks, both violent and intellectual, simply and stubbornly refuses to die. Perhaps, it's testimony to the fact that Indian culture was engineered at the outset with equal doses of wisdom and flexibility to navigate changing times and still retain its identity.

Indian culture today—our practices, rituals, heroes, stories, philosophies, food habits and worldview—is still largely based on millennia-old concepts, coming down from Vedic times and the dharmic principles of Hinduism, Buddhism and Jainism. It has been further enriched by the confluence of many influences over the last two millennia. Islam and Christianity may have come from the west, but they have been woven into the warp and weft of the culture of the Indian subcontinent very intricately. Through our history, we provided refuge to the oppressed from around the world; and, therefore, it is no surprise that Zoroastrianism and Judaism, among others, found a secure home here. We have rarely been nihilistic; we have almost always been accretive. Look at Sikhism, based as it is on our ancient dharmic philosophies, infused with new reforms.

In this book, through my articles and speeches, I have tried to answer Iqbal's question. What is it that makes India special? What is it about our ancient culture that still animates how we live today? What can we learn from our ancestors? And equally importantly, in what way can we be critical of our ancestors?

Through all these questions and answers, I try to explain modern issues facing India, the way I see it. For we are a relatively young country at seventy years. But our nation has the soul of an age-old civilization.

For most of human history, when our ancestors conducted the show, India was among the most powerful, wealthy, liberal and innovative lands on earth. We have had a few bad centuries. It happens. Many corruptions also seeped in, like the heinous caste system. It's time for us to learn from our ancestors, put our shoulder to the wheel, reform what needs reforming, build what needs building and make this country worthy of its history once again.

Having said all this, while I am conscious of the long road that we still have to travel as a country, and the need to question many things in India today, it does not take away from the fact that I am extremely proud to be Indian. There is no other place in the world I'd rather live. There's no other place in the world where I would like to die. And even in my next life, I'd like to be born right here once again.

Jai Hind. Glory to Mother India.

Religion and Mythology

Lord Shiva: The God of Contradictions

Lord Shiva was described by one of my younger readers as the Dude of the Gods. One may wonder, what makes Him so popular with the modern man and woman? He is, after all, an ascetic in a tiger-skin skirt, who smears himself with ash, drinks bhang with His ghoulish friends in His free time, and dances in cremation ghats. Does this sound like a 'cool' God? It appears contradictory, right? But being contradictory is His way. And therein lies the secret behind the immense devotion He generates.

Allow me to digress a bit and bring to your notice a long-dead English author, Charles Dickens; actually, a line from his book *A Tale of Two Cities*: 'It was the best of times, it was the worst of times.' It might well have been written to succinctly describe our present world. We live in times of complex contradictions, which furthermore, are wrapped within conundrums! In some sense, once again, it can be said that these are the best as well as the worst of times. Women have far greater rights today than they have had in, well, millennia, and yet crimes against women are unabated. Religious liberalism is being forcefully championed in a world that is connected as never before; technology and curiosity has resulted in a healthy dialogue between different faiths and yet, religious fundamentalism is tearing the world apart.

Perhaps for the first time in human history, the poor can legitimately dream of a lifestyle that was previously unthinkable and yet, our break-neck speed of economic growth is threatening environmental collapse. Social media has brought the whole world close and our life is seemingly cluttered by people and yet, too many feel desperately alone. Sex seems to pervade the media and public space and yet, people are ridden with a terrible sense of guilt regarding sensuality and desire. We are surrounded by massive public displays and celebrations of love, but the emotional succour that simple, but deep, unheralded love brings seems to be missing.

Yes, these are times of intense change and contradictions.

Is it any wonder then that the God who can shepherd us in such times would also be the Lord of contradictions? Of course, He wears clothes that none would don in polite society, but He's also the originator of many art forms that are beloved to the elite. He is the Nataraj, the Lord of Dance. Mythology holds that the Neelkanth revealed the secrets of Indian classical music to Maharishi Narad. He drinks bhang, an intoxicant that reveals to the mind an ethereal world, but harms the physical body. At the same time, He is also Adi Yogi, the originator of yoga, the path to physical, mental, emotional and spiritual balance. He prefers coarse, unpolished and even macabre companions and yet, the respect and love with which He treats His wife is a lesson in nobility. He's an ascetic, the ultimate Guru of renunciation who'd rather keep the material world at bay. But the erotic love he shares with His wife is the stuff of lore. His representation, the Shiva Linga, is regarded by many as the phallic symbol of creativity. He is an anti-elitist God who's always on the side of the disempowered, dispossessed and those who are on the fringe. But the most powerful kings have built massive temples dedicated to Him. As the originator of the Vedas, He has the intelligence of the ages and yet, His childish innocence makes His devotees lovingly call Him Bholenath. While one may fear His 'Rudra roop', the proprietary love of His devotees remains undiminished.

Why would a God be so contradictory? Because that is what we need.

He attracts us. And then He balances us.

The aristocrat is attracted to Lord Shiva as He is the Lord of the arts. And if the aristocrat is a true devotee, he will learn sensitivity towards the dispossessed from the Mahadev. A commoner is attracted to Lord Shiva as He behaves as if He is one of them. But the commoner would, over time, learn from Lord Shiva that he too can aspire and achieve; like the legendary Kannappa Nayanar. The Mahadev may attract the marijuana-smoking man, but if he is a true devotee, he will delve deeper into the philosophy of the Neelkanth and learn that yoga and spirituality can give him a greater high. And an ex-atheist like me gets pulled into the world of Lord Shiva because … He wishes it. He treats His devotees with respect, and as I developed a deeper understanding of the stories of the Mahadev, I learnt that the Lord wants us to respect all religions and Gods.

Many times, in order to balance our frenetic lives to find peace, we have to embrace contradictions. I have found my balance and peace through my devotion to Lord Shiva. I hope you find it as well.

First published in *The Week*, 2012

Playing It by the Rules; Lord Ram's Path

One of the privileges of being a writer on mythology is that one gets invited to literary festivals. At one such gathering, I found myself fielding tough questions on religious philosophies and personages. When there was a reason to criticize a narrative, I did so unhesitatingly. And when an opportunity presented itself to clear a misunderstanding, I attempted it with equanimity.

One exchange saddened me. While explaining a philosophical idea, I used the example of Lord Ram. A lady friend spoke with me after the event. I know her, as well as her religious and liberal beliefs. She asked me why I used the honorific 'Lord' for Lord Ram. I said I respect Him. I worship Him. It gives me satisfaction to honour Him. She said that she sees me as a liberal who respects women; then how can I respect Lord Ram, who treated His wife unfairly? She went on to make some very harsh pronouncements on Lord Ram.

Sadly, it has now become almost fashionable in liberal circles to criticize Lord Ram. In Hinduism, we are encouraged to question; Lord Krishna very clearly enjoins it upon us in the Bhagavad Gita. We are advised to form our own opinions on everything, even in theology and on God. But before we crystallize our opinion, we are also encouraged to think deeply and examine all aspects of the subject. We may be failing in our efforts to do this regarding Lord Ram.

Lord Ram is known as the 'Ideal Man', which is understood by most as the English translation of the Sanskrit phrase, *'Maryaada Purushottam'*. But this is an incomplete translation. 'Ideal Man' is the English equivalent of the Sanskrit word, *'purushottam'*. But what about the other word, *'maryaada'*? It means honour or rules or customs. So if we bring *'maryaada'* and *'purushottam'* together, then the correct translation in English is the 'Ideal-Follower-of-Rules'.

Let us dwell upon the role of the Ramayan and Mahabharat in Hindu scriptures. These two epics are not included in the Shrutis which are divinely-revealed philosophical texts like the Vedas and Upanishads. The Ramayan and the Mahabharat are called *itihasa,* a word that loosely translates as history. They are stories which tell us 'thus it happened'; they reveal archetypes and ideas that we can learn and derive wisdom from. And Lord Ram is the archetypal 'Ideal-Follower-of-Rules'. So what do we learn from the life of this 'Ideal-Follower-of-Rules'?

We learn that such archetypal leaders are transformative for their society as a whole. They create the conditions for their people to prosper and lead happy, contented lives. It is no surprise that the reign of the 'Ideal-Follower-of-Rules' continues to be regarded as the gold standard for benevolent administration: *Ram Rajya.* Sadly, while such archetypal leaders are good for society, they tend to struggle with their personal life. More often than not, the family of an 'Ideal-Follower-of-Rules' faces a challenging life; the 'Ideal-Follower-of-Rules' himself leads a rather sad life. Of course, we are all well aware that Lady Sita suffered abandonment by Lord Ram. I am not belittling Her suffering at all. Yes, He was unfair to Her; unequivocally so. He was also unable to be fair to

His children who were deprived of a father in the initial phase of their life. But how many of us know that Lord Ram suffered as well? He ended his mortal life with *jal samadhi*, essentially forsaking his body by drowning. Legend holds that as Lord Ram walked into the Sarayu River, in His last moments, He chanted the name of His wife: 'Sita, Sita, Sita.' Yes, He was not able to keep His family happy; He was not happy Himself either. Rules bring order to society; but within families, primacy of rules over love, is usually a path to unhappiness.

Do we know others from history or myth who walked the archetypal path of the 'Ideal-Follower-of-Rules'? Were there other enlightened leaders who may have greatly inspired the people they led, but whose personal life, as well as that of their family, was full of pain?

How about Mahatma Gandhi? He united our nation in a peaceful struggle for independence. He taught Indians, nay, the world, that violence need not be the answer. We revere him today as the Father of the Nation. But not only did he struggle in the role of a father, he also faced challenges as a husband to Kasturbaji.

Let's consider Gautam Buddha, one of the greatest Indians ever. He left behind a body of philosophical tools that continue to guide hundreds of millions of people in negotiating the challenges of life. His kindness, His compassion, and wisdom are worthy of worship. His Middle Path is worthy of instilling discipleship. But He too struggled as a father, son and husband. He walked away from His wife Yashodharaji and son Rahul, in search of enlightenment. In fact, the very name He gave to His son was indicative of His developing ideas on human bondage; Rahul translates as chains or fetters. He accepted Rahul in His sangh only when he renounced his rights as a son and became just another monk in the order.

Contemplate deeply upon these great figures. We have every reason to love them, for they sacrificed their own lives so that we could lead a better life. Had we been their family, though, we may have had cause for complaint.

And now tell me. What do you think of Lord Ram?

I, for one, am very clear. And I say it without any hint of embarrassment: Jai Shri Ram. Glory to Lord Ram.

First published in *Hindustan Times,* March 2014

Happily Religious and Liberal

I am a Shiva devotee. And I'm as devoted as they come. It's no surprise, therefore, that in my puja room at home, I have an idol of Lord Shiva placed in the centre. Alongside, of course, there are idols of other Hindu Gods, like Lord Ram, Lord Krishna, Lord Ganesh, Lord Kartik, Durga Maa, Kali Maa, Parvati Maa, Saraswati Maa, Lakshmi Maa, and many others (we Hindus have many Gods!). Equally importantly, you will find images of the Ka'aba, Mother Mary, Jesus Christ, Gautam Buddha, Guru Nanak, Prophet Zarathustra, and the Star of David. I worship and revere them all.

My friends quip in jest that I'm hedging my bets; ensuring that I am blessed by 'God', regardless of which one is the 'true religion'! But I'm only being true to the culture of my country.

In my teenage years I was an atheist; I remained so for many years. The recurring communal riots of the early 1990s had put me off religion itself. My devout father had tried explaining to me that religious extremism cannot be combated by secular extremism, for any form of extremism does not work. Countering religious intolerance with secular intolerance only replaces one monster with another. I didn't understand the import of my father's words at the time. I do now.

The answer to religious extremism lies in religious liberalism. This leads one to the next obvious question: what is liberalism? Modern Indian public debate has distorted the definition of liberalism. Being liberal is often misconstrued as being Leftist. But many Leftists are as illiberal as the Right-wing extremists they oppose.

The best definition of liberalism is brought forth in a statement that has been popularly, albeit incorrectly, credited to Voltaire; it was actually written by Evelyn Hall: 'I disapprove of what you say, but I will defend to the death your right to say it.'

How does this translate into religious liberalism? Very simple. I have my true religion and you have your true religion. I will respect your right to follow your truth and you must respect my right to follow mine.

Liberalism must be enforced by the elite (and at times mandated by the Constitution) if the society is, at its core, bigoted. In fact, we have observed this phenomenon in many societies. Not so in India. At our core, we are a society that is religious and liberal. In fact, it can be said that we go beyond Evelyn Hall's ideational template. We don't profess to 'tolerate' religions that we internally 'disapprove' of; we actively respect and embrace religions that are different from our own. The *Rig Veda* encompasses this philosophy beautifully: *Ekam sat vipra bahuda vadanti*—Truth is one, but the wise men speak (or know) it as many. The Muslim Manganiyars of Rajasthan sing devotional ballads based on the Ramayan without feeling any less Islamic in doing so. The Mount Mary church in Mumbai warmly welcomes Hindus, Muslims, and all other communities besides the Christians, providing them the freedom to fashion their own ideas of prayer and piety. Consider Ajmer Sharif, the tomb of a Muslim Sufi saint, thronged year after year by visitors from all communities of India. Consider the joie de vivre generated by Diwali, which is truly celebrated as the festival of lights by Christians, Muslims and Hindus.

This is precious and it must be cherished in India: the ability not just to respect but celebrate other religions, while being anchored to one's own. We have to understand that religious extremism will only be defeated by religious liberalism, not by ivory-tower, secular homilies from our elite.

We are faced with many social problems today; many of them are the result of centuries of societal decline. I believe that religious liberals—especially those who remain apolitical—can help resolve many of the issues that confront us. People will change their regressive social attitudes more easily if they feel their religion asks them to do so.

Women should not be in positions of power? Really? Listen to the magnificent tales of Shakti Maa and change your mind. Women should not conduct religious ceremonies or be part of a spiritual discourse? Read the debates between Maharishi Yajnavalkya and Maharishika Maitreyi in the *Brihadaranyak Upanishad* and realize how wrong you are. Women should not work? Then how does one explain the fact that Prophet Mohammed's wife, Khadija al-Kubra, was a businesswoman and the Prophet worked for her before He married her. The caste system based on birth is divinely ordained and cannot be challenged? Read the tales of Maharishi Satyakam and Maharishi Valmiki, learn from them and attack the caste system as it exists today. You are not supposed to question religious instructions or ancient traditions that don't make sense? Not true. Read the deeply profound chapter eighteen of the Bhagavad Gita and use your own discretion to make decisions, as Lord Krishna instructs you to. Honour your elders, even if they are wrong?

Our scriptures say something different. The *Taittiriya Upanishad* clearly states: 'Honour those who are worthy of honour.'

Religious liberals can alleviate many of India's social problems. And it's easy for us since we are a vast majority in our country. Unfortunately, we have abdicated public discourse to both secular and religious extremists. We must rise. We must speak loudly. We must bring out the liberal interpretations of our respective religions. It is our patriotic duty!

First published in *The Asian Age/Deccan Chronicle,* 2013

Inter-faith Dialogue

The Parliament of the World's Religions recently extended an invitation to me to speak at an event, my allotted subject being: 'The role of the youth in inter-faith dialogue'. I thought to myself: why not ask the youth what I should be speaking on? After all, they would know better what their role should be, compared to a forty-year-old like me.

So I met some students. And it was, I must admit, an interesting conversation. Some youngsters nonchalantly remarked, 'Inter-faith dialogue is a good idea and you oldies keep up the good work while we get on with our lives.' Another young man had a laid-back response and said, 'The trick is to look upon each other as friends, and not as Hindus or Muslims or Christians or Sikhs...'

I understand that some among you, who are thoughtful, may consider these responses simplistic. But the fact is that many people approach religion simplistically (though their approach towards other topics may be more thoughtful). Most people don't actually read the scriptures of their own religion (let alone those of other faiths). They just know a few rituals, which define their religious life. Given this reality, these simplistic suggestions may just work.

One observation from a young man, though, set me thinking. He said that we should encourage inter-faith marriages on the condition that neither husband nor wife convert to the other's faith. He felt that this way, many can discover faiths other than their own, perhaps see some similarities and equally likely, some divergences. And that it is all right that there are differences, for it is impossible for different religious systems to be exactly similar. But the couple will learn, in an intense manner, to live with diversity. He said that even within the same faith, including those that claim One Truth, there are different sects and interpretations. It got me thinking ... there may just be a deep philosophical idea embedded in that young man's thought process.

My suggestion is that we set aside the point on marriage, which should ideally be based on love, not on religious similarities or differences. But the key idea is this: religions are 'dissimilar', and this need not be a cause of worry.

Perhaps herein lies the problem with many inter-faith dialogues. There is discomfort with differences. Often one detects an almost desperate attempt to prove that 'We are all the same'.

Let me try and convey my perspective by using the human body. The nascent source of our anatomy is the same. In what way? Well, we are all carbon-based life forms made from the same chemicals, in the same proportion, with water being one of the primary components; so you see, the source is the same. And when we die, after a period of decay, our bodies return to the same chemicals that we emerged from. So in a way, the 'source' and 'destination' of every single human body is the same. But does that mean that our physical forms are exactly the same today? No. Some are tall, some are short. Some are fat, some are thin. Some are fair, others are dark. We have arisen from the same, and will end, also, in unity, but we remain different today. We cannot force a Potemkin similarity.

It's the same with the soul, the spirit. The source may be the same. The end may also be the same. Because both the beginning as well as the end is with God. But as we are today, we are spiritually different. Religion and spirituality aim to assist the journey of the soul. Since we are different today, our journeys will also be different. Some souls may find the path of Hinduism inspiring, some Islam, some Christianity, some Buddhism, some Sikhism or another faith. Some may even be inspired by atheism. That's okay. We must walk the path that resonates with our soul.

We must understand that our paths will be different. All cannot walk the same path, practice the same religion or even the same so-called 'universal values'. Consequently, we must refrain from judging another's path, or force-fit similarities where none exist. We need to learn to respect differences. It's not a competition. We shouldn't just 'tolerate' other religions, but respect them as well. I respect your path, and you respect mine (this is important though: respect must be mutual and not a one-way street).

So then, what is the point of inter-faith dialogue, if not to find some elusive similarities between all religions? Why do it at all? I think one should do it to satisfy that human quality that is at the very root of our uniqueness: intellectual curiosity. As we seek to learn about other lives and life forms, we should also seek to learn the different paths to God. No strand of wisdom is a waste. It plays a role in this great journey that our souls have undertaken. In this life. Or in the ones to follow.

First published in *Hindustan Times,* September 2015

Living Mythology

Myths are born. And then they die. It is the way of everything in the universe, and it would seem that even the Gods can't prevent it. Thor has been banished from Scandinavia, Ra's sun has set in Egypt and Zeus lies buried in the snow at Mount Olympus. But the myths of Lord Ram reign strong in India, Lord Krishna continues to entice and the magnificent Mahadev Lord Shiva has not ceased to dance in our hearts. An Akhand Ramayan reading in an Indian household slows time down even in these busy times. And people all over India never tire of dissecting the confounding characters of the Mahabharat. Why is this so? Why are most ancient civilizations left with merely the soulless shell of their mythological heritage, while in India we remain endlessly animated by the vibrant kernel of these millennia-old memories that continue to guide our everyday lives?

A lazy analysis might suggest that our myths are rich in comparison. But I would guard against this hubris. No doubt, they're delightful. But so are the Greek myths of Zeus and his cohort from Olympus; and just as magnificent and profound in their meaning. The hammer-wielding Thor was an inspiring figure from Norse mythology (some believe that Thursday's root is actually Thor's day). Why did these powerful Gods retreat into anonymity? Why are they, for all practical purposes, dead?

I believe it is because they lost their relevance in the lives of their people. Why? Because the Gods did not modernize and keep pace with their devotees. The myths of the Olympian Gods were relevant to the ancient era. But by the first millennium of the Common Era, as the influence of the Semitic religions grew, the stories of Zeus and his family remained unchanged, while the Greeks had modernized. Their old Gods no longer seemed free-spirited and passionate, but decadent and debauched. The evolving Greeks were unable to love and honour their Olympian Gods; in effect, this 'killed' them.

Why did this not happen in India? I think it was due to our genius for modernizing and localizing our myths. Let me elucidate my proposition with one of our most popular epics, the Ramayan. A television serial in the 1980s modernized Lord Ram's story to our age. It was based largely on the Ramcharitmanas written by Sant Tulsidasji in the sixteenth century. But Tulsidasji himself made significant changes from the original Valmiki Ramayan, thus modernizing the story of Lord Ram for the time that he lived in. The *Kamba Ramayanam* from the south, localized the Ramayan to the sensibilities of the Tamilians of the twelfth century. There are possibly hundreds of versions of the Ramayan across Asia, in which the core thoughts have remained the same, but the body around it has been modernized or localized. The stories of our Gods have constantly evolved, retaining the best of the old, but adding in the attractiveness of the new, thus keeping our myths relevant, ever-contemporary and alive. And this is not just a Hindu trait; it's the characteristic adopted by all religions that are practised in India. Islam and Christianity, too, are localized, as is Zoroastrianism and Judaism. It's not uncommon to walk into an Indian church and find the image of Mother Mary dressed in a sari, like an Indian woman. Great Sufi saints employed local Indian myths and memes to preach the tenets of Islam.

In sum, the reason our myths stay alive is that unlike in most other countries, religion and liberalism have not been historically at war in India. Consequently, different religions have learnt to coexist and by and large, be open-minded; we celebrate modernization and localization, keeping our theology relevant, and hence, alive.

Counter-intuitively, it is possible for liberalism to feed religiosity and vice-versa. And our India, this beautiful country, has always been counter-intuitive!

First published in *The Times of India,* 2011

Unbridled Shakti

Lady Sati decided to enter my imagination through a novel interpretation in my book, *The Immortals of Meluha*. I visualized Her as a strong woman with a mind of Her own. Her husband, Lord Shiva, loves and honours Her as an equal. Are some elements of my conceptualization different when compared to popular myths that are remembered today? Possibly. But is there a tradition in Hinduism that imagines our mythological tales with bewildering variety, often with differing messages? Very strongly, yes. And they present the faithful with the choice of myth that resonates within their soul and gives them peace.

Let's step back a bit and dwell upon the treatment of women in India today. Despite the visible improvements in their status at a surface level, in many ways, our society is regressing. New technologies make it possible to commit crimes in a sanitized, seemingly 'non-brutal' manner—female foeticide is one appalling example of this.

Why do women still struggle for their rights in India? Increased education and wealth does not seem to make a material difference. Punjab, Haryana and Gujarat, for instance, have the highest rate of female foeticide. An important reason for this attitude is the use of a patriarchal prism to interpret our past and myths. Many may justify these crimes in their mind because 'our Gods, themselves, reveal to us that women are a source of trouble.'

However, the truth is that our resplendent tradition also offers a solid foundation for alternative insights, including the strongly matrilineal.

For example, while the hugely popular Tulsidasji's Ramcharitmanas (a sixteenth-century modernization of the original tale of Lord Ram) depicts Lady Sita as submissive and docile, the original Ramayan, scripted by Maharishi Valmiki, has a much stronger Lady Sita, portrayed as a woman with a mind of her own. The Lady Sita of *Adbhut Ramayan* (one among the hundreds of interpretations of Ramayan) is a fierce warrior Goddess. Even Lord Manu, the apparent torch-bearer of Hindu patriarchy, had espoused that 'where women are honoured, the Gods are pleased'. Perhaps liberal Hindus should highlight these alternative perspectives from the past to those who think a woman is inferior. A Deobandi fatwa makes it unlawful for Muslim women to find employment in mixed-gender work groups. Many non-Muslims may be unaware of the illustrious Lady Khadija al-Kubra, who ran a hugely successful trading business in ancient Arabia and donated large sums to charity. She would later marry one of the agents who worked for her, Mohammad Ibn Abdullah, a man who was fifteen years her junior; and her husband honoured and loved her. We know Him today as the Prophet Mohammad. Perhaps liberal Muslims should mention the example of Lady Khadija to those co-religionists who think women should be suppressed.

Our past offers us valid interpretations that can be powerfully used to end the historical and religious justifications for the ill-treatment of women today. And those of us who are aware of them, have a moral duty to speak up. The best way to bring about a change in human beings is to tap into the very beliefs that are central to their being, instead of attacking those beliefs. By respectfully showcasing an alternative perspective as to who we are, we allow for the flow of natural transformation. It is an organic, non-destructive evolution in which lies the gentle essence of life.

First published in 'The Speaking Tree', 2011

The Purpose of God

Hello and good morning, ladies and gentlemen. You know, this may come as a surprise to you but I find it very difficult to be unbiased and objective about Lord Shiva. I am very emotional about Him. I am, what some may call, a very ardent devotee of Lord Shiva. So when Kalli Purie (COO and the director of India Today Conclave) posed this question to me—Did Shiva Live?—my response was immediate and clear: of course He did. And Lord Shiva continues to live, He lives in my heart and He lives in the heart of every single Shiva worshipper. But this is an emotional, at best devotional argument; it's not intellectual. And this conclave is, very obviously, a gathering of intellectuals. So let me strain my grey cells to try and present an alternative, intellect-based argument.

What I said at the beginning, of my belief in Lord Shiva's existence, is I guess an expression of love and devotion; the path of *Bhakti Yog*. Let me try and walk the path of knowledge, of *Gyaan Yog*.

Before we debate about whether Lord Shiva lives, let's discuss the purpose of religion itself. What is its role? It exists across almost all cultures in some form or the other. More importantly, why does it persist so relentlessly? Atheists hold that religion is a weapon that the elite use to control the masses. Marxists famously espouse, 'Religion is the opium of the masses.' Honestly, I find that assertion ironic and silly, because Marxism itself often behaves like a religion. Its adherents frequently prefer dogma over intellectual rigour in forming their opinions.

The religious camp of believers has its own dogma. They tell you that religion is an organized effort to create an ethical society; there are studies (I must say) which can back this claim, for instance the behavioural studies conducted in the University of Austin. But there are problems with this argument as well. For instance, the ethical framework of the great religion, Islam, has been twisted by an insecure state like Pakistan to commit heinous crimes. And Islam is not the only religion which has been misused in this manner by a few to spread hatred and violence. It has happened to every religion, if not in the present times, then definitely at some time in the past, be it Hinduism, Christianity, Buddhism, Judaism, or any other religion. There is empirical evidence that they have all been misused at some point in history to spread hatred and divisions.

So where does that leave us? What *is* the purpose of religion? If I may suggest, let us look at how the ancient Indians approached religion. The *Katha Upanishad* is in the nature of a conversation between Nachiket, a young boy with a philosophical bent of mind, and Lord Yamraj, the God of death. Interestingly, Lord Yamraj was also the God of dharma. In fact, across many ancient religions, death and dharma went hand in hand. Coming back to the *Katha Upanishad*, the conversation between Nachiket and Lord Yamraj is so deep and meaningful that we can spend an entire lifetime decoding it. Regrettably, I do not have a lifetime on this stage, and I'll restrict myself to a part of that conversation. It is said that while nearing the end of the exchange, having received wisdom most profound from Lord Yamraj, Nachiket became free from his passions and 'death'. He realized God, and so it shall be with anyone who knows God; for it refers to the Self.

Examine that thought for a moment. God refers to the Self. That was the purpose of religion in ancient times. It was to raise the consciousness of every human being and bring it in contact with one's inner divinity. Was this philosophical worldview uniquely Indian or Hindu? Not really; it existed across the ancient world. The Egyptian myths of Osiris, the God of the underworld, and Mahaat, the Goddess of truth and justice, are pregnant with esoteric meaning. The ancient Egyptians believed that the purpose of life was to prepare for a meaningful death, after having reached one's potential during a lifetime. Once that is achieved, then one lived among the Gods as an immortal. The ancient Mediterranean coast was dotted with schools of mystery, one of which was steered by the brilliant mathematician and philosopher, Pythagoras. The greatest bequeath from Pythagoras was not the Pythagoras theorem (the theorem was, by the way, discovered earlier by Rishi Baudhayanaji); it was actually his school of mystery. They believed in the concept of the Microcosmos, Mesocosmos and the Macrocosmos. Microcosmos represented the human being. Macrocosmos was the entire universe and divinity. Mesocosmos was society, and its purpose was to raise the consciousness of the Microcosmos and unite it with the Macrocosmos. In simple terms, the purpose of society was to bring the human into contact with his/her divinity. Sounds familiar, right?

At the root is the concept of unity; that the *Parmatma* and *Jeevatma* are one. Plato had pithily instructed: *Know Thyself.* Sri Aurobindo said that the great lesson of the Upanishads is *Atmanam Vidhi*, know your true self and be free. If we agree upon this as the true purpose of religion, then what is the purpose of God? With due apologies to Dylan Thomas, is God supposed to sit on a sad height that we can't even aspire to reach? Or is God a role model who dwells among us and who teaches us through His example what we are capable of becoming. There was another Dylan who wondered: how many times can a man turn his head and pretend that he just doesn't see? The answer, my friend, is blowing in the wind. God is a role model, He moves among us, sometimes as Jesus Christ and the Christian Trinity, at other times as Gautam Buddha, and other times as Lord Krishna, Lord Ram, Goddess Durga and yes, as my God, Lord Shiva. And His karma is so grand that He continues to live. He lives in my heart and in the heart of every single Shiva worshipper. Thank You.

India Today Conclave, March 2013

Recasting Mythology

Q: I want to talk about *The Secret of the Nagas*, about Ganesh and Kartik. You have put them across beautifully as differently-abled people. What made you do that, because a lot of us in modern India have now started to see differently-abled people as those with some unique, special features? But putting Ganesh and Kartik as huge warriors was also brilliant. What was the thought process behind it?

A: Firstly, on the issue that medication can sometimes impact the body in drastic ways ... I think the idea came from something I'd read in the *Scientific American* journal a long time ago. A medicine was discovered in the 1950s and '60s, thalidomide, which was considered a miracle cure for morning sickness. As I am sure you are all aware, morning sickness is something that women face during pregnancy. If there are dedicated husbands here, I'm sure they would also recall the collateral impact of morning sickness. So, thalidomide rapidly became a very popular drug. But it was discovered a few years later, that a few children whose mothers had taken thalidomide, were born with some chronic and serious physical issues. Many had deformed limbs, for instance. Others were born with malfunctioning hearts; some were visually or even hearing impaired. Thalidomide was subsequently banned.

So a very strong medicine can do good for some and also cause serious damage to others, including making some differently-abled. That was an idea that remained in my mind and helped inspire this idea in my books. And as for Lord Ganesh and Lord Kartik being warriors, well they are great warriors in our traditional myths as well!

Q: While writing this book, you admitted that you did lots and lots of research. So during your research, you may have come across Ram, Ramayan and Ayodhya a lot of times. So do you think that Ayodhya or Ramayan existed? Or do you think it was folklore which was modernized and put together again and again, like a bestseller. Maybe your books would have sold twenty-five million, and fifty or a hundred years down the line, people would think this was what Shiva was like. So basically was it fact or mythology?

A: I think the best way to answer this is to understand what is mythology and what is history. There are mythology-loving cultures and history-centric cultures. On an average, mythology-loving cultures tend to be more liberal. How do we differentiate mythology from history? Historians will say their submissions are based on 'facts'. If you disagree with them, they will either deride you or ridicule you or sometimes, sadly, even boycott you. There have been many in history—not historians—who even say their truth is 'THE Truth' and if you don't agree, they might even kill you. But mythology-lovers tend to instinctively respect different points of view. And they believe that perhaps there is no One Truth, but many, depending on the perspective of the observer. A technical term for this is observer-bias. Even science is increasingly accepting the phenomenon of observer-bias, for instance in theoretical physics. Mathematics is perhaps the only stream where One Absolute Truth is possible. In maths, 2+2 is 4.There is no interpretation or other Truth possible. Many ancients believed that maths is the language in which the Gods wrote the universe. But in every other subject, there are many interpretations of the possible truth. To paraphrase Nietzsche, there is your truth and there is my truth; as for the universal truth, no one knows what it is. Mythology-lovers readily tend to accept this because they are used to many interpretations of the same story, and they love and accept all versions. So, having said all this, what is my approach to the Ramayan? I believe that our Gods existed. I believe that they were our ancestors. I believe their blood flows in our veins. Therefore, I obviously believe that Lord Ram existed. I believe that the Ramayan, or some events similar to it, did happen. Can I prove it? No. Am I trying to force it upon you? No. If you don't want to believe it, don't believe it. But I believe Lord Ram existed. And I believe He speaks to us, through the ages, through His story.

Q: At what stage does mythology become faith?

A: When you stop questioning. There is nothing wrong with faith as well. Faith begins when your knowledge reaches its finish line. Knowledge helps you grow; faith helps you make sense of things you don't understand. Or at least find some peace with it. But we are encouraged, in our ancient scriptures, repeatedly, to question. In the Bhagavad Gita, Lord Krishna tells Arjun, 'I have given you knowledge most profound, now it is your task to ponder over it and do what you think is right.' That is Lord Krishna's message to us. Because only *you* have to live with your karma. No one else. You have to decide whether your karma is in line with your *swadharma* or not. Basically, God has blessed you with intelligence and you must use it. You must question. You must think. And then come up with your own opinion.

Q: You have a fantastic way of delivering new-age mythology. What was the thought process when you started writing in the first place? Like Alex Rutherford added a lot of spice in history to give it that zing, you have also done the same thing. As a young Hindu said, we were quickly drawn into the books and looking forward for more. Millions of others have done it. So when you started, what was in your mind and did you want to bring that different angle to it so that millions of other Hindus or anybody else could understand mythology which people often say is most complex.

A: To begin with, I should make a clarification: you'll see this at my events, among my readers, that there are others who read my books, besides Hindus. Among my readers, you will find Muslims, Christians, Sikhs, Buddhists, Jains, Jews, atheists and many others. And to me, this is a sign of the innate liberalism of most Indians. I get emails and tweets from people of all faiths. In my puja room at home, of course, I have an idol of Lord Shiva at the centre, but I have idols of various other Hindu Gods as well. I also have symbols and marks of other faiths as well. I worship them all every morning. As for my writing, frankly, I didn't do any market research before I began to write my first book, *The Immortals of Meluha*. I just went ahead and wrote. I simply did what felt right to me. I wasn't thinking whether this book would be received well; whether critics or readers would like it. I had thought, in all probability, the only ones who would read my book would be my family, the captive audience! And even with *Scion of Ikshvaku*, the first of the Ram Chandra Series, I have written in a similar spirit. I think about the audience only in the marketing phase, not in the writing phase. And I am very clear that if my next book flops, I'll go back to banking. But I will write what feels right to me. On that I am very clear.

Q: You have depicted two great Indian Gods, Lord Shiva and Lord Ram. Someone like me has grown up seeing Lord Ram as an ideal, and we have idolized Him in many ways. There is a lot to learn from our Gods. But during the period of colonialism they were not portrayed well. And this impacted our culture negatively. Sadly, sixty years into Independence and I am afraid we have not learnt our lessons. Do you think we are again losing it by not portraying these mythological stories well so the new generation can learn contemporary lessons?

A: My suggestion is to be a little patient. A country doesn't change rapidly. You must cultivate a sense of time from the perspective of a nation, and not your own individual life. Let me make this point through a thought experiment, if you will: imagine you are a housefly who lives just for a few weeks, and you are born during the monsoon season in India. You would 'know' that India is all about unending rain and not much else; especially if you lived in Mumbai or Cherrapunji. But, as a human being, who will live for seventy-eighty years, you know that the housefly is technically correct, but only from a limited perspective. The longer the timeframe, the more 'whole' the perspective. My suggestion is that you look at the life of a nation the same way. Six to seven decades seem like a very long time for a human being, but for a nation which could have a 10,000-year life-span, it is not so long. Changes in a nation take time. We just need to see that we are moving in the right direction. Broadly, I would say, yes we are. Of course there are problems, and I have spoken about many of them publicly. We Indians have had a few bad centuries. It happens. But we are emerging again; we are waking up. Especially after 1991. There is a return of our historical, argumentative confidence. I am a very proud Indian. And going forward, our country will give us more and more reasons to be proud. Let's be patient.

Times Literature Festival, Delhi, November 2015

The Masculine/Feminine Way and Other Questions

Q: Amish said he wanted the official Q&A to be as short as possible. He wanted to let you (the audience) ask him more questions. I think he wants the session to be more interactive. The basic topic of discussion is whether Ram is easier or more accessible to young readers than Shiva. *Maryada* vs *Tandav.* Is Ram a more acceptable role model for younger readers than Shiva? That's what I take it to mean though I am making a value judgement here and Amish is strongly against value judgements. But you know the concept of *maryada* first of all. Your Ram is most of the things that Valmiki's Ram is and yet He goes beyond certain concepts of morals and honour. He maintains all of that, but He is also very human. So what is *maryada* according to you? How do you see it?

A: Good question. Look, the theory in my books is that there are two ways, two balancing points between which society keeps swinging. One is the paradigm of freedom, of passion, of individuality and the other is the paradigm of compliance, of truth (or at least an interpretation of the truth), of justice and honour. And both these ways of life have their own strengths and weaknesses. The problems begin when you start judging either of the two. Lord Ram's way, the way of *maryada* is obviously the Suryavanshi (or Masculine) way, a path of honour, of truth, of justice; and Lord Krishna's way is the Chandravanshi (or Feminine) way, the path of freedom, passion, individuality. And Lord Shiva is impartial to both these ways of life. I should clarify that when I say a way of life is Masculine or Feminine, it has nothing to do with men and women. It's about a way of life. There are many men (not just women), who follow the Feminine way, and there are many women (not just men), who follow the Masculine way. These are the traditional concepts I explain in my books. I'm not suggesting that any way of life is better or worse. They are just different paths, that's all. One shouldn't judge.

Q: He keeps saying this. He makes it very difficult.

A: No, I don't! (*laughs*) Okay, let's look at it this way then. No person or community or country is ever completely Suryavanshi (Masculine) or Chandravanshi (Feminine). There are shades of both, but usually one is predominant. China, I believe, follows a way of life that is closer to the Suryavanshi path. Now, you know China staged the Olympics in 2008, right? The Beijing Olympics; which was, all will agree, nothing like the Indian Commonwealth Games. I've been told that the Chinese stadia were actually ready a good six months to a year before the Games began. In India, I believe, they were painting the stadia even as the games were being inaugurated. But for China, just having the infrastructure ready on time wasn't good enough. They decided that they must impress the visiting countries, so they gave certain guidelines to the volunteers who worked at the Games' venues: how to talk, dress, etc. Which is fair enough. But even that was not good enough for the Chinese government. They also gave guidelines to the citizens of Beijing. I'm not kidding. How to greet foreigners, tips on communication and such like. They even prescribed dress codes. Again, I'm not joking. There were, I was told, different dress protocols suggested for women and men. For example, men were told not to combine white socks with black shoes, for some reason. God knows why. So what do you think the citizens of Beijing did when these guidelines were issued? I was told that the guidelines were followed; there was compliance. Now, conduct this thought experiment: what would have happened had the Indian government prescribed such guidelines?

Q: In India… *(starts laughing)*

(*Audience starts laughing too*)

A: You would have probably heard the following: '*Tumne bola safed moze kale juttey ke saath nahi pehno? Mein ek saal tak yahi pehenunga!*' (You tell me not to wear white socks with black shoes? I will wear only this for one whole year!) That would probably be the Indian reaction. Why? Because we are, at least at this stage, more of a Chandravanshi country. We are a rebellious people. We are a freedom-loving people. But the corollary is that we are also a passionate and creative people. That is our strength. We should be true to who we are today. We should not try to be like the Chinese.

Q: So … *tandav*?

A: Having said that, I am not suggesting we take our rebelliousness to an extreme and not respect any laws; as we do today. We should be true to who we are. But, we can also learn from Lord Ram to respect laws. It leads to a better society. We can learn from Lord Ram that it just might be cool to follow rules; sometimes at least. I don't recommend chaos born out of unbridled freedom with no restraint or the constant disobeying of the law. There must be balance. And the wisdom of the Indian way of life is, and always has been, to try and strike that balance. Extremism of any sort should be renounced.

Q: When *Scion of Ikshvaku* was released … Ikshvaku in itself is a word you don't hear too often. A few know that Ram belonged to the Ikshvaku dynasty. But it was almost a revival of this term. For lots of people who are not so familiar with the texts, who only know the bare bones of the Ramayan and the Mahabharata (and there are lots of such people whether they admit it or not), Ikshvaku is not a very familiar name. So what made you select this as the title of your book?

A: Till a century ago, Lord Ikshvaku was a very well-known name. Sadly, our education system has slowly cut off many Indians from their roots. Everyone here, I am sure, knows of the 1980s television serial on the Ramayan. In it the word used often for Lord Ram's royal dynasty was Raghukul, i.e., the clan of Raghu. Of course, Lord Raghu was also an ancestor of Lord Ram. But the founder of the dynasty was Lord Ikshvaku. Also, I like the name. I think it has an attractive ring to it. Moreover, it has a very sweet meaning. Ikshvaku means the one who speaks sweetly. So I thought it's a good title to have.

By the way, do you know what the word Ramayan means? Ram is (as you well know) His name. What does the word ayana mean?

Q: I don't know.

A: It can be interpreted as travels. Ramayan is, literally, 'the travels of Ram'. That's one of the translations of the word Ramayan.

Travelling is an educational experience, and it was even more so for the ancients. So Ramayan, in a way, is the making of the God whom we came to respect and I daresay, love. It's about how He learnt and evolved and eventually became the God we know.

Q: My next question was—is it actually possible to become a God, transcend your mortality?

A: But that is actually the Indian concept. The difference between the Gods whom we worship and us is that they have discovered the God within, while we are still at it.

Q: Okay, I think that's a very good answer. Which brings us to somebody we already know as a God, an established God. Shiva. He's part of our trinity, He's the Destroyer, He's a rebel. He is this ash-smeared, ganja-smoking, completely untidy person. Why are the youth even going near him?

A: In fact, you just described why the youth will go to him.

Q: Well my question was a joke. I was trying to be ironic.

A: Well, one of my younger readers described Him as the Dude of the Gods. And I mean no disrespect to any other Gods.

Q: No, no, of course not, He is an Absolute ... So how did such a person become a God in the first place? Is the deification of Shiva ... Can you just take us back because I know you read a lot. Your research is way ahead and much more than most of us here. I can sort of say that with some certainty. What lies at the root of His Godliness? How did Shiva become a God in the Aryan pantheon? In the documented Hindu pantheon, how did Shiva find His way in? Because He is clearly not an Aryan God.

A: In fact, there are serious debates about whether there ever was a race called the Aryans. In the *Rig Veda*, the term 'Arya' is used only once. And that too, not in the context of a race. So far as my knowledge goes, there is no credible archaeological evidence of any invasion 3,500 years ago (when the Aryans had supposedly invaded India). Modern genetic research has blown serious holes in the theory that a new race marched into India 3,500 years ago. 'Arya' was simply a term of respect, that's all. So I don't think there were Aryan Gods or Dravidian Gods. They were all Indic Gods. Also, I think the Shaivite way and the Vaishnav way again represents two different perspectives of life. If I have to explain the two approaches in a simplistic manner, it would be like this: the Vaishnav way is working within this *mayavi* (illusionary) world and finding a sense of purpose and order within it, along with the discipline of self-control. The Shaivite way is about neither resisting nor being obsessed by the *rasas* (pleasures or delights) of this *mayavi* world. You can enjoy them, but ultimately you will need to move beyond them and discover detachment. I admit, these explanations are a very simplistic way of looking at two very deep sets of philosophies. Of course, as you go deeper, you will realize that they're far more complex. But both of them are valid and appropriate paths. You walk the one that inspires you personally. There's no right and wrong in this.

Q: How did you actually place Shiva in any context? You know when you wrote about Him, your Trilogy, you did, in some of your interviews, state a chronological context. How did you place Him in that place and time?

A: His placement at around 1900 BCE was linked to the dying of the Saraswati river. Some scientific studies indicate that the river perhaps died out somewhere between 2000 and 1800 BCE.

Roughly around 4,000 years ago. My story was closely linked to the dying of the Saraswati river.

Q: The question clearly remains, when you were writing about Shiva, you humanized Him. You had to first internally humanize Him and then express Him for our benefit. And because your stories are written in such an accessible way, I had no trouble identifying with a very humanized version of Shiva. Though to be honest, as I was saying, He possesses more human qualities than most of our other deities. You know we have kept Him firmly grounded.

A: According to our scriptures, He is the only one from among the Tridev, the holy Hindu Trinity, Who actually lives on earth. He lives on Kailash mountain.

Q: So what is it about Him do you think, that draws us?

A: I think it's His contradictions that draw us to Him. But specifically for someone like me … I am by nature a rebellious person, slightly anti-elitist. I was an atheist for ten-twelve years, in my early youth. So for someone like me to return to faith, the best God to return to is Lord Shiva. Because He Himself is a very rebellious God. He is the God of the rebels. He also dances brilliantly, He is the God of music, He loves his wife passionately. He's the Adi Yogi as well. Yes, He is very cool. Once again, no disrespect to any other God.

Q: Since you brought up the subject of his beloved wife, let's talk about the women of the Shiva Trilogy as well as the first book of the Ram Chandra Series, *Scion of Ikshvaku*. You have a tendency, you gravitate towards very strong women characters, attributing them with far more than they started out with in the original epics; you know Sati, Sita. What is this tendency towards these warrior princesses that you seem to favour a lot?

A: Firstly, I guess personal experience. My family is populated with strong women: my mother, my sister, my sisters-in-law, my wife; these are not women who brook any nonsense. It's the standard model I am used to. We are three brothers and one sister, my sister being the oldest. My parents did not differentiate between the boys and the girl while we were growing up. The rules were the same for us all. Secondly, let's look at our epics. Many of the versions of the epics that most urban Indians are aware of, at least in the modern day, are based on television serials from the 1980s. And many of them were based on late medieval interpretations of our epic stories. Yes, most late medieval interpretations of our epics tend to be patriarchal. Any society which has faced a lot of violence tends to become patriarchal. It's a natural sociological process. And India did suffer horrific violence in the medieval era. But if you study the versions of our epics, of our myths, from an earlier era, it would not be so out-of-the-ordinary to find very strong women, and interpretations that are not patriarchal. For example, in ancient times, the highest status in society was accorded to the rishis; it was even higher than that of kings. You could equate them (sort of, but not exactly) with the prophets and messiahs of the Abrahamic faiths. They communicated with the divine and decoded that knowledge for the common people. Now, many hymns in the *Rig Veda* are written by rishikas, i.e., women rishis. There's a version of the Ramayan called the *Adbhut Ramayan*, which is also credited to Maharishi Valmikiji. Sita Maa kills the elder Raavan in that version when she takes her true form as Maa Kali.

So my stories, with very strong women characters, I would suggest, are more true to our ancient way.

Q: I don't mean to be rude or offensive. But I feel some times we look at Ramayan very, very simplistically. We were talking about it earlier, about how complex things are. Don't you think it's us or those that preceded us that demonized Raavan and deified Ram? Honestly speaking, to me it sometimes appears like the war of two kings. Would you like to comment on that?

A: You are not being rude by asking this question. Do you know there is a temple in UP dedicated to Raavan. And the worshippers of Raavan also respect Lord Ram. There is a place called Mandsaur on the Rajasthan–MP border, where they worship Raavan and his wife, Mandodari. There is a very famous story wherein, as Raavan lay dying, Lord Ram asked His brother, Lord Lakshman to approach Raavan and learn from the great intellectual. The battle may have been fought, but Lord Ram respected some qualities in His enemy. The idea of Raavan being a purely demented evil demon is, again, relatively modern. In the traditional Indian concept, there is no pure good and pure evil; it did not exist at all. In ancient Sanskrit, there is no exact translation for the English word, 'evil'. I wrote the Shiva Trilogy to explain the concept of evil. But had I written in Sanskrit, there would be no need for explanation because the concept of evil didn't exist. Nothing is pure evil. Everything exists for a purpose. In the ancient versions of the Ramayan, the portrayal of Raavan is quite nuanced, his positive attributes too are exemplified. It was called *Sone ki Lanka*, right? Why? Because he was a good king for his people. He had faults as well, primarily his ego. So we can learn something from Raavan too. This simplistic approach of viewing things in black or white terms is actually quite modern; it's not our ancient way. Life is never simple. Real life is complicated. Our ancient stories reflect this reality.

Q: But why is Ram deified?

A: But in the Indian way, all of us are deified; all of us are potentially divine. The true journey is to learn from our Gods how we can deify ourselves. How can we discover the God within? It's actually a very powerful concept. It's not about an external God who will 'judge' you. It's about looking at God as a role model and learning, so you can become God. That's the true journey. So then, asking that question is a bit like talking about football when we are actually playing cricket. Why stop at just deifying Lord Ram? Why not learn from Lord Ram and discover how you can find the divine within yourself?

Q: I have read the Shiva Trilogy and also the first book of the Ram Chandra Series. So we deify Ram and call him the *Maryada Purushottam,* but in your book you have shown it brilliantly. I have no words to describe it. Shiva is the person who brings together the Chandravanshi and Suryavanshi ways of life. He unites them into a code of life which is very much balanced. So why not call Shiva *Maryada Purushottam* and we give Ram some other title?

A: You are assuming that *Maryada Purushottam* is a higher or lower title. It's not. It's just something to learn from. The words—*maryada* and *purushottam*—refer to a life of laws. That's what it's supposed to mean. There are other ways of life as well. As Lord Shiva, the Mahadev, His mission is not to advocate any way of life; He's beyond all that. The Mahadev's mission is to remove evil from the equation. This is why Lord Shiva cannot be biased towards anyone. This is why He has to belong to everyone.

And as has always been said, Lord Shiva and Lord Vishnu work in partnership for the good of all. There are enough tales in all our scriptures of the respect that Lord Shiva and Lord Vishnu have for each other. Having said that, I think there is a lot that we can learn from Lord Ram, the *Maryada Purushottam*. In modern India, we take rule-breaking a little too far. We could perhaps learn from Lord Ram that we must follow rules. Our society would become a little more efficient, and a little less chaotic, if we at least try to follow some rules.

Q: I have been following all your books and I would like to know where the story of Ram's sister comes in?

A: There is no version of the Ramayan that I have read which mentions Lord Ram's sister. But there is a reference to Lord Ram's sister in the Mahabharat. I've been told there is a sister in some regional retellings of the Ramayan as well. So it's an interpretation. My version of the Ramayan is an interpretation from various other versions, some back-stories from the Mahabharat, and some stories from the Puranas, all mixed with my imagination.

Q: Thank you for introducing the concept of religion to the youth who say they are atheists and don't want to talk about religion. There is this new phenomenon of youth actually coming up and discussing Shiva and Ram. So for starters, thank you for that. My question is: as a Bengali, everybody in my house is crazy about Michael Madhusudan Dutt who wrote *Meghnad Badh Kavya,* in which he speaks about Meghnad being the hero and showing Raavan's good side as well. I have been brought up in that kind of a background and although I haven't grown up to oppose Ram, but it has always been instilled in me as a pattern of thought that Ram and Raavan showed two different sides, but each was complementing the other. Your comment on this view.

A: The first thing I want to say is that there is nothing wrong with atheism. In ancient India, we had various schools of philosophy, *darshana*. Of these schools, some were devoted to the path of atheists. The Charvaks, for example, were atheists. It's better to be a good atheist doing good karma, as compared to a religious extremist doing bad karma. So don't judge atheism. In the traditional Indian way, there was no question of oppressing atheists. Now, coming to your question of approaching the story from the perspective of Meghnad and Raavan and the relationship between Lord Ram and Raavan. You know, there is a very popular myth in UP, at least in the area that my family comes from and about which I have spoken earlier. When Raavan lay dying, Lord Ram sent Lord Lakshman to meet him and learn from Raavan because he was a great intellectual and his knowledge of the arts, of administration, of the Vedas, and of philosophy was exemplary. Lord Lakshman approached Raavan even as he lay wounded, but he stood by Raavan's head and the latter refused to speak. So Lord Lakshman returned to his brother and complained. Lord Ram then approached Raavan, but He stood by his feet. He showed him respect. And He gained knowledge from the learned Raavan. Which brings us back to the point I made earlier, that the idea of Raavan as this unadulterated, demented, evil demon is a relatively recent phenomenon. It wasn't the way the ancient Indians, our ancestors, approached Raavan or any other subject.

Q: You were discussing about two types of icons, *Maryaada Purushottam* and of course the *Tandav* of Lord Shiva. But in the

Ramayan, there are also very strong associations between Ram and Shiva. First of all, both are one-woman men; they do not believe in polygamy. Then of course, Lord Ram wins Sita by lifting the Shiva dhanush. So I think, they are also associated with each other.

A: Lord Ram was a Shiva bhakt as well, just like many of us are. And so was Raavan, by the way. And Lord Shiva respected Lord Ram tremendously too. We know the story of Rishi Agastya, right? There's another story in which Lord Shiva tells Parvati Maa that if She is unable to recite the complete version of the *Vishnu Sahasranam* (the 1,000 names of Lord Vishnu), She can just chant the name of Ram, for it has the same power. Lord Shiva and Lord Ram respected and worshipped each other. You are right.

Q: We've heard that in Raavan's early life, he was a Shiva bhakt and one of the most ardent devotees of the Lord. And in the end, he does certain things that are not justifiable. So at what point did he turn from good to bad? And if we encounter such a point, how do we stop ourselves?

A: In the Indian worldview, there is no concept of you being good or evil. It's about karma and its consequences. So you encounter the consequences of your karma: 'good' or 'bad'. And this is not just so for human beings, it happens to the Gods as well. If you do something that is not in line with dharma, then karma will come back to you. What we must do is learn. From Raavan, we understand the perils of an almighty ego; how the ego can destroy you. To a certain extent, I suppose the ego is probably good for you. For example, if you belong to the underclass and you are fighting a system that is elite-driven, which makes it difficult to break through, the ego is probably good because it gives you the drive to keep pushing ahead. But invariably, there comes a point in life when the ego is harmful and a block. You have to find that balance within yourself.

Q: I just want to know what kind of research you employ when you write about science in the Shiva Trilogy, when you write about imbibing the *somras*, planning for the battles and all that. Where do you get your source material from?

A: I just read a lot. At a minimum, I read at least four-five books a month. And I have been reading at this pace for decades. In my family, everyone reads a lot. We also debate a lot. We are a typical Indian family in the truly traditional sense. There is nothing that cannot be discussed, that cannot be questioned. So most of my learning comes from reading and discussions within my family.

Q: What I am asking is, are the scientific portions in your books actually true or are they speculations? Did ancient India really have such sciences?

A: Look, in my books there are some things which are of course conjured up. There is no proof that there were nuclear weapons in those days. There was some paper presented at the World Science Congress recently that we had travelled to Mars; there is no proof of that either. But the problem is that our education system is such that we know very little about our own ancient legacy and particularly, our scientific achievements. I have mentioned it even earlier, about a very high quality paper which was presented at the same Congress claiming that an Indian, Rishi Baudhayanaji, discovered the Pythagoras theorem before Pythagoras did. That is actually a fact. It finds mention in the *Shulba Sutras*, which is credibly dated 200 years before Pythagoras. This is something that even the Europeans have accepted. Surgery was practiced in ancient India. It's in the *Sushruta Samhita* (as evidenced in the Bower Documents). Possibly the earliest recording of a rhinoplasty surgery in the modern era was done a few centuries ago in India, on a soldier in the Maratha army. The surgeon was a barber! The surgery was recorded at the time by two British men in *The Gentleman's Magazine*. And that barber-turned-surgeon followed the exact procedure as laid down in the *Sushruta Samhita* more than a thousand years ago. *And* that surgery was successful. Modern rhinoplasty still follows a variation of that surgical process. Now, why do fantasies associated with our scientific past, like the supposed space travel to Mars, exist in India today? It's because there is an absence of genuine knowledge. Speculative theories proliferate in an environment of ignorance. We teach practically nothing about our own past scientific achievements in our schools! Our medical education begins with Greek medicine; we don't teach Indian medicine. Our mathematical education focuses on the Western development of maths. We don't learn anything about Indian mathematicians, who are among the greatest in history and have produced seminal work. We need to teach ourselves about our own achievements. We need to draw inspiration from them. And build an achievement culture today that will make us worthy of our great ancestors.

Tata Steel Kolkata Literary Meet, February 2016

How the Shiva Trilogy Ended and Other Questions

Q: Is a popular novel always a classic, or being popular is one of the qualities of a classic novel?

A: Not all popular novels become classics, that is obvious. But yes, over time it's difficult for a novel to become a classic, if it's not read widely, which by definition means popular. The true worth of a novel is not determined by immediate popularity or immediate critical acclaim, but time. If your novel is alive even after a hundred years, it's a classic novel, or else it is not. This idea is exemplified by the Hindi word for 'classic': *kaaljayee,* which translates as one that has defeated time. A classic is a novel that even time could not kill.

Q: How would you judge the qualities of a writer?

A: This is best left to the readers. A writer should aim to be genuine, true to himself. While writing, he should not be concerned with critics, publishers or readers. He needs to be true to himself and write with honesty.

Q: What is your opinion about the manner in which ancient history is treated in India?

A: I have said this before and shall say it several times over. It's a matter of deep sadness that our education system leaves most Indians with very little knowledge about our ancient past. And I am not talking about stories of a few emperors, but our ancient sciences, arts and philosophies. These are simply not taught to us. In this atmosphere of ignorance about our past, two groups of extremists control the narrative: one set that believes in fantastical tales like Indians having undertaken inter-planetary travel to Mars, of which there is no proof. And then there is the other group that refuses to accede that ancient Indians achieved anything at all. They deride ancient India and believe that there was no excellence worth noting, which again is not true. We had made great scientific, mathematical, medical, architectural, agricultural and other achievements. Ancient literature, music and arts also need to be studied in an open and unbiased manner. Very rarely is a country the inheritor of such great heritage and yet remains ignorant of it. Our present educational system needs drastic reform.

Q: 'A novel is an impression, not an argument.' Should we be guided by this assertion of Thomas Hardy in our acceptance of the character of Shiva? The diverse aspects of typical Indian mentality and Indian life are reflected in Shiva. What is your opinion in this regard?

A: The traditional Indian way was to encourage different points of view, and to respect them. In ancient India, the Charvaks were atheists; even the Samkhyas and the Mimansas were atheists in the modern sense, as they believed in the Vedas but not in God. Despite the differences, they didn't get attacked. There was no violence. There would be debates, of course. They were comfortable with contradictions. Therefore, a novel is the presentation of a point of view and you can think about it. If you agree, great, and if you don't, come up with your own perspective.

Q: Shiva or Mahadev, who plays the central part in the Shiva Trilogy, represents a great ancient character, reflecting innumerable and limitless (positive/negative) possibilities. Did the character-traits of Shiva, as we observe at His initial appearance, continue till the end? Why did Shiva decide to explode the 'Pashupatastra' in the final phase of the novel? The grace and beauty of the character maintained throughout the Trilogy seems to be shattered by that very decision towards the end of the work. How would you explain this?

A: This is a question that has been put to me by many readers. And before I answer this specifically in the context of the Shiva Trilogy, I would request that we step back and examine the traditional Indian storytelling style. Ancient tales very rarely had an ending that offered a sense of conclusion or denouement. Unlike modern Bollywood films which usually give you a closure; whether it be a happy ending or sometimes, even a sad ending. Some say, this style of storytelling emerged with the Bhakti movement in the medieval era. In this style of storytelling, you have an ending which gives you a sense of closure; then you tie a neat little ribbon around the story and put it away on a memory shelf, and very rarely go back to it. Ancient Indian storytelling was usually different. The ending was NOT designed to give you a sense of conclusion; in fact it aimed to unsettle you and leave you troubled. You should be left with more questions at the end than you had at the beginning. This perspective throws light on the endings of the Ramayan and the Mahabharat, two of our greatest epics. They left us with such serious questions at the end, that we continue to wrestle with them, even millennia later. Why did Lord Ram abandon Lady Sita, committing both Her and Himself to life-long sadness and tragedy? What were the Kauravas doing in heaven at the end of the Mahabharat, while all the Pandavas fell into hell, albeit temporarily? All except Yudhishtra; so why was he spared the descent? What was the point of the Dharma Yudh? Now these are endings which leave you with very good questions.

Storytelling in ancient India aimed to communicate philosophies, and not just leave you with a nice, warm, fuzzy feeling at the end. The best way to delve into philosophical ideas is to provoke questions at the end. Like all of us have questions about the Mahabharat or Ramayan. And then, in seeking answers to those questions, we discover philosophies and learn lessons we are *meant* to learn. Now, your answers may be different from my answers; even your questions may be different from mine, which is okay, because you are different from me. In this present life, you are meant to learn some lessons and I am meant to learn others.

If you approach it from this perspective, then what are the questions which emerge at the end of the Shiva Trilogy? If you allow me the indulgence of suggesting some questions… Does anger serve the cause of justice? If so, why? If not, why not? If you want to explore this idea a bit, read the works of Plato, the Mahabharat by Rishi Ved Vyas, and the tales of Lord Shiva in His Rudra roop in the many Shaivite Puranas. There is an even more fundamental quest: what is justice? There is human-centric justice and there is Mother Nature's concept of justice. The human concept of justice is often adversarial, but Mother Nature's justice is about restoring balance. Another question: what makes a good leader? And how do you judge whether a leader was effective or not? Is it based on the impact derived from his/her actions in the immediate present or in a period spanning several years or decades? Think about Lady Sati; everyone will agree that She was very morally right at the end of the Shiva Trilogy. But in Her moral certainty, She led her own loyal people to their gruesome deaths. Would you call that good leadership? If not, why not? If yes, why? I am not providing answers; I am just throwing up ideas to ponder over. Think about Lord Shiva. Why did He do what He did? And what are we supposed to learn from His actions? It's essentially about questions. The idea of constantly evaluating and passing judgement on everything is a relatively modern pursuit. In ancient times, people were more interested in learning rather than judging; and then applying the lessons to their own lives.

I have to make a confession—even I am troubled by the ending. At the time of writing, I had another ending in mind which would have probably given the readers of my book a sense of conclusion. But somehow I was clear that that can't be the ending. It had to be what I wrote finally. Maybe, sometime in the future, I'll release that other ending… But understand this, the purpose of the ancient Indian style of storytelling is to leave you deeply troubled at the end because that is when you set out on a quest, ask questions, find answers and learn philosophies for your own life.

Q: The Shiva Trilogy is set in a period which can be defined as the breeding time of human civilization. The land, people, society, civilization and culture of Meluha during that prehistoric period, as reflected in your splendid narrative, maintain a standard that corresponds to our modern times. But was such human progress possible during that initial period of civilization? Isn't it but a fascinating creation of your imagination?

A: While some parts of my books are based on verifiable historical facts, I can't say the same for other things that feature in my writings. So I am not claiming it's the truth; only Lord Shiva knows the truth. But all I'd like to say is that we may stand well advised to not imagine arrogantly that we are at the high point of human civilization. There is enough evidence that various civilizations have seen many ups and downs. Perhaps we can learn from our ancestors as well. They also achieved great things in some areas; there can be some knowledge systems where they were ahead of us. And if we have some humility, maybe we can learn something from them.

Q: Anyone can raise oneself to the stature of God or Mahadev... Does heredity or family tradition play the role of a catalyst in this regard?

A: This is a done-to-death debate: nature or nurture? I am not suggesting that heredity has no role to play, but I believe it's a small role. A large part of what you achieve in your life is determined by your own choices and circumstances, and how you react to what life presents you with. Some people receive the best upbringing and yet achieve very little, if at all. And others may face adversities, with the world not making it easy for them, and yet they achieve a lot. The way I look at it is that a lot of what happens to you is essentially in your own hands; you can take charge of your life. So ultimately, it is you that determines what your life is.

Q: 'The purpose is not the destination but the journey itself. Only those who understand this simple truth can experience true happiness.' At a time when widespread consumerism has taken almost all the corners of our contemporary society into its grasp, how would you like to illustrate the deep significance of this eternal line from the Gita?

A: It is something we need to learn. We are destroying the earth with our consumerist exuberance. We are ripping Mother Nature apart. It might even have been remotely worthwhile if all this consumerism was leading to some happiness. But data suggests that excess consumerism is not leading to happiness. In fact in hugely consumerist societies like America or Europe, you find so much loneliness and unhappiness that it's heart-breaking. So we are ripping the world apart and not even gaining happiness out of it. It's so ironical and so sad to see what we are doing. We need to find a balance. Happiness comes from within. It doesn't come from external life or the stuff you acquire.

First published in *Dainik Janambhumi,* 2016

Beliefs May Be Cast in Stone

My wife and I finally saw the much-talked-about movie, *PK*. Let us first be done with the obvious: I oppose calls for banning the movie or *violent* protests against it (non-violent protests, of course, are legal). If in the past I have opposed the ban on *The Satanic Verses* and *The Da Vinci Code* (banned in some Indian states) then I must abide by the same standards for *PK*.

Let us now use the same *freedom of expression* standards to pose some questions to the filmmakers of *PK*. Clearly, *PK* is a noble attempt to convince us that naked, humanoid aliens regularly visit India and they can educate us on our relationship with God. In this same spirit of scientific inquiry, *PK* casts some serious doubts on religion. Actually, not all religions; some have been covered perfunctorily. The primary scholarly analysis is on religions that practice idol-worship (Note that, theologically, practically all idol-worshippers are also nature-worshippers, for their philosophical undergirding is common).

PK is clearly making 'rational' arguments against those who love myths, follow living spiritual masters (as opposed to prophets/messiahs who lived many centuries ago) and worship idols. You may imagine that only Hinduism answers to this description. You would be wrong. Idol-worshipping cultures proliferated across the length and breadth of the world in ancient times; and most encouraged questioning. Nothing was beyond the pale of critical examination because they did not believe in only One Truth. Certainly, there are features of Hinduism that can and should be questioned. But, intriguingly, the makers of *PK* thought it fit to pass judgement on some strengths of idol-worshipping cultures instead.

The fact that idol-worshipping cultures, normally, have living spiritual masters allows them to change easily in tandem with fast-changing times. Reform is, more often than not, easier for such cultures and you will find that among them, philosophies and core ideas adapt relatively smoothly over time. Admittedly, there are some unsavoury elements among the present-day spiritual masters. But the 'Muslim terrorist', the 'paedophile Christian priest' and the 'unscrupulous idol-worshipping godman' have a common thread—they all suffer from the fallacy of stereotyping. Maybe I'm naive, but one expects intelligent filmmakers to be nuanced enough to not stereotype godmen. Especially when their film itself argues against stereotyping Pakistani men as terrorists.

Consider a 'hard-hitting' scene in the movie. The protagonist picks up a rock, applies *paan masala* on it, and says that soon this will become God whom everyone will worship. The subtext is clear: Look at these idol-worshipping idiots who will worship anything. Don't they realize that this is not the real God, who apparently is an 'external', 'other-worldly' entity?

This belief that idol-worshipping is somehow wrong, or at least primitive and tribal, has been around for long. However, few are able to give a cogent theological answer as to why it's wrong; except one that you can't argue with: 'My God said so!' Over the last two millennia, some communities, such as the European Christians and the Turkic Muslims, took this dislike to an extreme level in their zeal to end the 'Satanic' idol-worshipping practice forcibly. There has been massive violence across the world to purge idol worship. Many places of worship were destroyed, others appropriated, and millions of people slaughtered simply because they worshipped idols. The ancient world was dotted with idol-worshipping cultures. But today, most of them—the Hellenic, Khemit, Mesopotamian, etc.—have been exterminated; those ancient Gods and Goddesses, along with their archaeological and mythical remains, serve a utilitarian role today, as focal points for the tourism industry and for research by the academic world. Hinduism is a rare idol-worshipping culture that has survived as a lived experience. Interestingly, I have not come across many historical instances of idol-worshipping cultures going around the world killing 'others' simply because they were not worshipping idols.

I am not suggesting that idol-rejecting cultures are 'bad'; there are strengths and qualities in them; weaknesses as well. Similarly, some weaknesses afflict the idol-worshipping way of life, and some strengths too. But there is one immeasurably precious quality that idol-worshipping cultures possess; which is the secret to their inherent liberalism. Surprisingly, this is precisely what is portrayed in *PK* as a weakness viz.: that idol-worshippers are open to worshipping anything, even a stone.

What is the philosophical idea that underpins this attitude? Why are we willing to worship anything? Because this might lead us to subtly see the divine in everything. There is nothing in this world that is not divine or Godly. This gives someone like me the philosophical grounding to worship Gods/symbols of all faiths. It gives us the theoretical framework to be able to love and respect everyone, even those among the idol-rejecters who hate us simply because we worship idols. Because we see God in them as well. This gives us the potential ability to respect nature and the environment with religious zeal, since we don't believe that nature was created for our use, but that it is God!

What transforms a stone into God? Our belief does it. Can this belief be exploited? Possibly. But precisely which human belief is sealed off from the possibility of human exploitation? In any case, if as shown in the movie, some pray to a stone, and if this gives them hope, then what exactly is the problem? Hope is one of the greatest human strengths, the one that refused to leave even Pandora's famous box! And how is worshipping a stone different from someone visiting a temple with an officially recognized idol, or a mosque or a church? You will think there is a difference only if you believe God doesn't exist everywhere and in everything. If, like me, you're a nature- and idol-worshipper, you will find that God is everywhere. In you, in me, in animals, in trees and yes, even in that stone in the movie *PK*.

First published in *Hindustan Times*, January 2015

Different Ramayans. Different Sitas.

I was in Cambodia recently, visiting the temples of Siem Reap. The main attraction, of course, was the Angkor Wat. Massive bas-reliefs carved onto the walls of the temple, tell many a story from Hindu religious traditions. Among these is a sixty-metre-long, beautifully carved gallery, depicting episodes from the Ramayan. If you happen to visit, look closely at the way the characters have been depicted. Lord Ram is not the dark-skinned Indian described in our versions of the great epic. In fact, he looks Cambodian.

When the story of the Ramayan travelled to Cambodia, many centuries ago, they made it their own—in every way. Change is natural when one travels across space and time, right?

The word Ramayan itself simply means the 'journey of Ram'. There is of course an allegorical and deeper meaning to the word 'journey'. But the story of Ramayan, is also, in a way, the physical journey of Lord Ram—from Ayodhya, into banishment, to Lanka, and back to Ayodhya. Quite like Lord Ram's journeys, his story, the Ramayan, has travelled to many places too. Not just in India, but beyond its boundaries as well.

And, as is natural, the story has changed hues as it has travelled.

Consider the many versions prevalent in the Indian subcontinent. The version that most urban Indians think of as the original Ramayan is actually a 1980s TV serial. Created by Mr Ramanand Sagar, it largely used the Ramcharitmanas as its source material. Are there differences from the original Valmiki Ramayan? Of course there are.

And that is the beauty of the dharmic way. Whether it is practised here in India, or abroad (in areas such as Southeast Asia), all of us have a right to approach dharma in our own way. All of us have a right to see Lord Ram and Lady Sita in the way that inspires us.

In one of the Buddhist versions of the Ramayan, called the Dashrath Jataka, there was no abduction of Lady Sita at all. Lord Ram, Lady Sita and Lord Lakshman were simply sent to a hermitage in the Himalayas for twelve years. In the Jain version, on the other hand, Lord Ram was completely non-violent, and it was Lord Lakshman who killed Raavan. In the Malay version of the great epic, Hikayat Seri Rama, Lord Lakshman has a much larger role, almost like a parallel hero. In the Thai version of the Ramayan, called Ramakien, Lord Hanuman is given huge importance. In fact, the great Monkey God is the most popular character in the story for many Malaysians. I've been told that in Myanmar, their version of the story, called Yama Zatdaw, is like the unofficial national epic. And in the Indonesian versions, indigenous deities, like Twalen, have also been included in the story.

So how has Lady Sita been seen across so many of these epics? Since most of us rely on the 1980s TV serial, we believe in a certain image of Lady Sita. Words like 'docile' and 'submissive' are often used to describe her. What we need to remember is that in many other versions of the Ramayan, she is radically different.

In the Valmiki Ramayan (which is the original version of the Ramayan), she is a much stronger character. She is a woman who knows her mind and will fight for what she thinks is right. In versions like the Gond Ramayani and Adbhut Ramayan, Lady Sita shows her warrior side as well. In fact, in the Adbhut Ramayan, the elder Raavan (who is the main enemy) is actually killed by Lady Sita, not Lord Ram; this was when Lady Sita took her Maa Kali form.

What many of these versions teach us very clearly, is that to respect and idolize Lady Sita, we do not have to disrespect Lord Ram. In fact, we can, and must, worship both. This is a distinction that often gets lost in the modern day.

These ancient versions, which show the stronger side of Lady Sita, have also been hugely popular in history. But their popularity declined in the last few centuries, especially in the time when India faced horrific and brutal attacks from foreign invaders.

I think the time has come to see Lady Sita in her ancient avatar once again—that of a strong woman; an adopted child who rose to become a warrior prime minister and then a Goddess. *Dharma* and *maryaada* must be respected. But *Shakti* does not have to be sacrificed for that to happen.

Let's revive our ancient Indian way. Let's celebrate *Shakti*, the feminine power. We need it now. More than ever. For as our ancient scriptures say, the Gods abandon the land where women are not respected.

First published in *Mumbai Mirror*, May 2017

Mahakaleshwarji: The Great Lord of Time

Prime Minister Narendra Modi will inaugurate the Mahakaleshwar temple project in Ujjain, one of our most ancient cities, on 11 October 2022. It is a significant event in India's journey as a civilizational state. You may wonder, why? We present to you two reasons:

The first is faith-based and devotional in content. Mahakaleshwarji is one of the great Jyotirlingas dedicated to the worship of Lord Shiva. Thousands and, on ritual days, lakhs of devotees gather at the temple to pray to Mahadev. The temple had faced iconoclastic attacks in the past and, in modern times, illegal encroachments around its precinct. Skanda Purana mentions the Rudrasagar Lake close to the temple, which woefully had become a shrunken sewage dump.

But now this great temple is rejuvenated. The Madhya Pradesh government cleared encroachments peacefully after discussions with residents, with suitable compensation. It helped that the residents understood the fillip the local economy would receive as a result of the proposed renewal. Traffic decongestion in the core city, parisar expansion and decentralized parking, safety and security hardware and software, intelligent pedestrian circulation and crowd management protocols, coupled with artful aesthetics, have combined efficiency with beauty. Green measures include e-rickshaws with adequate charging docks providing noise- and pollution-free quick transport while solar panels meet electricity demand.

Inside too, as I realized during a visit a fortnight ago, it's a breathtaking transformation. Beautiful panels using traditional techniques to depict stories of Lord Shiva are all around. Stunning life-like statues of Lord Shiva and Goddess Parvati with their children Lord Ganesh and Lord Kartikeya tug at your heartstrings. Sculptures and graven images of Shiva–Parvati vivah, Tripurasura vadh, Tandava swaroop and the Saptarishis beam you into a mystical state. Rudrasagar Lake has been restored to its pristine form with waters from the holy Shipra River nearby. Facilities for the thronging pilgrims are state-of-the-art. It's a devotional renaissance.

A second aspect is in play in Ujjain today, a holographic repatterning that is built into the name of this great temple: *Mahakaleshwar* as Lord Shiva is the *Great Lord of Time*. Ujjain—Avanti of old—was an ancient centre for scientific research. Celebrated mathematicians and astronomers like Varahamihira, Brahmagupta and Bhaskaracharya travelled from distant regions of India and made Ujjain their home. This was because the city was considered home to the prime or zero meridian—a reference point for the calculation of time by ancient Indian mathematicians and scientists. Today, a brass strip at the Royal Observatory in Greenwich in the UK represents zero meridian.

Ujjain is also considered by early astrologers as the spot where the Tropic of Cancer—Karka Rekha—intersects with the zero meridian. During the summer solstice—the longest day of the year—the sun is overhead at midday. It is the beginning of the period of Dakshinayana when the Sun God begins his journey south. It was, therefore, a logical location to anchor the calculation of time. No wonder the city was called the navel of the world. The Hindu lunisolar calendar—panchang—uses Ujjain as the zero meridian to this day. Most Hindu homes know the panchang as the eponymous Kaal Nirnay that keeps track of our festivals and ritual days.

Ujjain is the home of Mahakaal. And this is not an accidental occurrence. In ancient times, the overhead sun on summer solstice fell directly on the *shikhar* (tip) of the spire atop the grand Mahakaleshwar temple. It might have diverted by now to the nearby Mangal Mandir (temple of Mars). This would occur due to the precession of the earth's axis. Remember that fascinating geography lesson from school—that the earth wobbles on its axis? Broadly, though, it is the same location as was described in the ancient astronomical text from the fourth century CE: Surya Siddhanta.

This re-infusion of energy into the temple precincts will hopefully also lead to a revival of our sciences and exploration of our ancient texts created in and around Avanti. In the play *Julius Caesar*, Brutus informs Cassius that there is a 'tide in the affairs of men' that must be 'taken at the flood'. It 'leads on to fortune'. How beautifully Shakespeare captures the essence of time with those famous words. Time is an energy which, if not used, wastefully dissipates never to return. Time moves inexorably, trapping us in its inevitable forward movement. And yet, if we can seize time and pull it in the vertical direction of this moment, we can grab the baton thrust into our extended hand by our ancestors. And spur our wonderful nation into a glorious future.

Written with Bhavna Roy; first published in *The Times of India*, October 2022

The Ram Janmabhoomi Temple

The Ram Janmabhoomi temple will be rebuilt. It will be grand and magnificent, a testimony to the glory of our great God, Lord Ram. We will worship there. We will honour Him there. We will celebrate our culture there. But is that all that we must do? Is that all that we owe Lord Ram, one of the greatest that ever walked this earth? Let us think a bit about it.

It is interesting that in all the versions of our wonderful epic, the Ramayan, very little of the text is devoted to what Lord Ram is most famous for, i.e., Ram Rajya or the Rule of Ram. The story usually centres around the struggles of Lord Ram, usually up to the time when he comes back with Goddess Sita after defeating Raavan and rescuing her. Some of the philosophies that Lord Ram seemed to subscribe to (and would therefore implement in his rule) are discussed in texts such as the *Yoga Vashistha*. But in the main text of the Ramayan, it is largely his story up to the time he returns and becomes the king, and perhaps a quick summary of events thereafter in the *Uttara Kand*. Ram Rajya is not discussed in too much detail. Even the word Ramayan literally means the journey of Ram. But in the hearts and minds of practically all Indians to this day, the term Ram Rajya evokes powerful memories; like a talisman for our souls. It is the basis of our love and respect for Lord Ram. If you ask around in the country what is the best way to administer a kingdom, regardless of the religion, caste or linguistic background of the Indian being asked, practically all would say, Ram Rajya.

There can be various theories on why the term Ram Rajya is so viscerally felt among most Indians, many, many millennia after Lord Ram, but yet, there is little discussion of it in the Ramayan. Perhaps governance discussions are boring, but battles and love-stories are made for epic tales! Few readers of the Mahabharat would list the governance lessons in *Shanti Parva* as among their favourite sections. Or maybe Indians of that era already knew of the contours of Ram Rajya and were interested in only listening to the journey of the great God who actually set it up. But another possible explanation appeals to me. Maybe each era has its own Ram Rajya. The Indians who lived in Lord Ram's time experienced their own concept of Ram Rajya. And our ancestors decided that their descendants must make up their own minds on what Ram Rajya should be. Therefore, our tradition dictates that we must all think, ponder and debate, collectively, on what Ram Rajya can mean in today's times.

Seen from this perspective, the various versions of the Ramayan are an inspiration for what we can be; how a leader should or should not be; how a people should or should not be. And most importantly, what is the central thrust of what we, collectively, as a society, hope to achieve.

But a discussion on Ram Rajya can only happen when we are clear about who we are. And this decision, rightly or wrongly, is usually taken by the ruling elite; the class that comprises the top politicians, bureaucrats, judiciary, academia, media, corporates, artists, etc. This ruling elite in India has, at least culturally, largely been the same for the last 150 years. They have been called *Macaulayputras*, the *children of Macaulay*, the cultural descendants of the thinker behind the British policies to create a class that was Indian in blood, but British in food, language and culture. The idiom this class uses, the cultural memes they follow, and the language they speak, are all, largely, an inheritance of the British Raj. That does not mean that they don't love India. Of course they do. It just means that their method of expressing that love is different; they see themselves as reformers of a land that is pre-modern (some among them use the term 'savage'). Once you understand this, you also understand how this class approaches everything Indian. And among the ancient Gods, the One that this class despised the most was Lord Ram; criticism of Him was almost fashionable among them.

But as Francis Fukuyama suggests in his book *Identity*, that we are driven by our tribal identities. And another tribe is rising today to take over as the ruling elite. For want of a better term, let's call them the *Dhartiputras*; the *sons of the soil.* Since the *Dhartiputras* are clearly the future, the conversation within this class is most important in India today. Like the *Macaulayputras*, this class too loves India. They are of course influenced by the dominant paradigm of the modern era: that of Western culture. But at the heart of it all, the idiom this class uses, the food they eat, and the cultural memes they follow, are usually based on ancient Indian traditions. And it is no surprise that this class idolizes Lord Ram. There is no unquestioning obedience, however; in the traditional Indian way, there is no concept of blasphemy. So this class questions Lord Ram when they think they need to, for example, on his treatment of Goddess Sita. But that does not take away from their deep and abiding respect for Lord Ram. Interestingly, despite that respect and worship, does this class learn from Lord Ram? We'll come to that in a bit.

Now, the *Dhartiputras* have not taken over the elite space completely. Their journey has only just begun. And even ideologically, they are a work in progress. Not everything is thought through. Some among them, even today, feel a visceral dislike for the *Macaulayputras* and see them as 'the enemy'. They waste too much energy fighting them. This is pointless. They should learn from the way Lord Ram treated others, even those who were 'His enemies'. And what they should learn even more from Lord Ram is that the important conversation is not what you do to your enemies; it is what you do for your people.

What should this class do for its people, i.e., us, common Indians? What kind of society do we want? What are the texts we should refer to? What is the Indian dream? What is our approach to science? What is our approach to women's rights? What is our approach to sexual and religious minorities? Do we believe in multiple laws based on group rights (as the *Macaulayputras* did) or do we believe in one law for all built on the foundation of individual rights and equality? What is the balance between economic growth and environmentalism? What is the balance between pacifism and resisting countries who do not wish us well? What is the balance between order and freedom? Do we believe in the concept of guilt for historical crimes? Do we believe in the concept of community guilt? What is our approach to education? To history? To the arts? To literature?

There is so much to be discussed. So much to be debated. And it must all happen in the public square. I try to discuss some of these questions in my interpretation of the Ramayan: the five-book Ram Chandra Series. I'd love there to be more debate. Perhaps those debates can happen in the to-be-constructed Ram

Janmabhoomi temple, in a spirit of investigation, mutual respect, and maturity. But more importantly, the debates should not be just talk. They must convert into karma. We must put those thoughts into action; the *dhartiputras,* maybe, along with the *Macaulayputras*, can all work for the good of the common people. Perhaps, sometimes, with disagreement, but preferably without being disagreeable. For that is what Lord Ram would expect us to do. For that is the finest way to honour Him.

Rāmarājyavāsī tvam, procchrayasva te śiram
Nyāyārthaṁ yudhyasva, sarveṣu samaṁ cara
Paripālaya durbalam, viddhi dharmaṁ varam
Procchrayasva te śiram,
Rāmarājyavāsī tvam.

You live in Ram's kingdom, hold your head high.
Fight for justice. Treat all as equal.
Protect the weak. Know that dharma is above all.
Hold your head high,
You live in the kingdom of Ram.

First published by Observer Research Foundation, November 2019

Social Issues

LGBT Rights and Section 377

Change happens when one is ready for it—be it at an individual or a societal level. And one arrives at this readiness through discussions and debates. It was heartening, then, to observe a few politicians from across the political spectrum take a liberal stand on the issue of LGBT rights. I believe it's time we debated Section 377 of the Indian Penal Code that criminalizes sexual activity of LGBTs (Lesbians, Gays, Bisexuals and Transgenders). It is an egregious and illiberal Section that must be repealed. There are some who have reservations based on cultural and religious grounds. Well, let's discuss them.

I am not as deeply familiar with Christian and Muslim scriptures as compared to Hindu texts, but we know that the Semitic faiths specifically ban homosexual relations, which are viewed as an abomination and a serious crime. But there is no uniform interpretation or approach. Muslim Saudi Arabia prescribes severe punishment, including the death penalty for homosexuality, while Kuwait does not criminalize lesbianism (though male homosexuality is still a crime). Christian Ireland, a country that bans abortions even in cases of pregnancies induced by rape or incest, has decriminalized homosexuality. I am sure liberal interpretations on the LGBT issue are possible and I leave it to Indian Christian and Muslim liberals to find them and speak out. Let me address the issue from a Hindu perspective.

Many stories from Hindu texts make a reference to LGBTs in a non-negative way. There is the famous example of Shikhandi from the Mahabharat, who proved to be the nemesis of Bhishma himself. King Bhangaswan was a man who later changed into a woman, comfortably exercising his freedom of choice. The founder of the great Chandravanshi clan, Ilaa, was born a girl. At one stage, she transformed into a man named Ila, and sired more children. Lesbianism finds mention in Vatsyayanaji's *Kamasutra*. I do not know of any story or text from ancient India in which a person was punished severely for his/her sexual orientation. Admittedly, at times one didn't find approval for it in the texts, but never was it singled out for strong disapproval or viewed as a serious crime.

No doubt, some may argue: what about Hindu community laws? What about the *Manu Smriti*? Firstly, we should know that the Smritis (or law books) were man-made and visualized as temporal, unlike the Shrutis (like the Vedas) which were revered as having divine origin. Compiled periodically to regulate society, there are numerous Smritis. The conservative *Manu Smriti* was given stark publicity by the British above all other Smritis, and presented as if it was the only one. But it's not; there are many others. The Smritis essentially reflected the collective mood of the times they were written in. Some Smritis are very liberal and some are conservative. We can write our own Smriti, at any point in time; in fact we've done so, recently. And the latest Smriti is called the Indian Constitution.

Having said that, let us examine what even the conservative *Manu Smriti* has to say about homosexuality. It was listed as a relatively minor misdemeanour; and the only punishment prescribed was a ritual bath with your clothes on. Interestingly, if a man cheated on his wife, it was considered a very serious crime, the punishment for which was the death penalty. So even the conservative *Manu Smriti* does not view homosexuality as an abomination. Culturally, ancient India had a liberal attitude towards non-mainstream sexual practices. Perhaps this was because sex itself was not embroiled in tortuous guilt. It was not an obsession either. It was just another beautiful aspect of this wondrous cycle of life.

Section 377 does not reflect the traditional Indian attitudes towards sex. It is, in fact, a reflection of the British colonial mind-set, influenced by medieval interpretations of Christianity. This attitude gradually seeped into the colonized people over the centuries.

Having said so, this cultural debate is, as it should be, an ongoing process in society. Laws on the other hand cannot, and should not, be circumscribed by religious or cultural restrictions. That is not the way a multi-religious society can create an efficient and stable State.

A liberal society is built on the foundation of respect for liberty and individual rights: none shall face discrimination from the law, and all can exercise the right to lead their life the way they wish to, so long as they don't force their choices upon others. However, the post-Independence form of Indian liberalism is a unique creature; it is more respectful of group rights than individual rights. Ergo, we have incorporated many sectarian laws into our statute books. As mentioned elsewhere in this book, Hindus have tax benefits that are not available to non-Hindu Indians through the HUF clause (also see Divide And Rule Laws in Modern India, page 151). Muslim women suffer injustices (such as polygamy and triple talaq) that their other Indian sisters don't. The Right to Education (RTE) Act, combined with the 93rd Amendment, specifically contains clauses that are inapplicable to Muslim and Christian educational institutions. There are many more such examples. Most modern Indian liberals do not find such sectarian laws odd because, I daresay, they have not imbibed the spirit of genuine liberalism and individual rights. A modern State can only be premised on individual rights, with no differentiation under the law on the basis of group or community entitlements. Hence, applying the principle of true liberalism, if heterosexual couples have the freedom to love each other, LGBT couples deserve it as well.

Let's be truly Indian. Let's be truly liberal.

First published in *Hindustan Times,* January 2016

On Religious Conversions

Of late, the issue of religious conversions has taken centre-stage, with emotions running high. The Christians argue that had their efforts at harvesting souls through conversions been strong and widespread, they wouldn't constitute merely 2.3 per cent of the population. Muslims claim they do not indulge in organized conversion efforts and the growth in their proportion of the Indian population, from under 10 per cent in 1951 to nearly 14 per cent, can be attributed to poverty and a higher birth-rate. Hindus, reduced in proportion from over 84 per cent in 1951 to 80 per cent, state that their non-proselytising culture works to their disadvantage, so they have every right to *ghar-wapsi* (literally meaning home-coming, but in this context returning to the fold) programmes.

Perhaps it's time to dump the emotions and take a rational look at the issue.

In all honesty, while there may be material gains from religious conversions, spiritually, it is almost always negative. Why? Because spiritual growth happens with internal focus, when you attempt to seek truth within yourself; not when you try to prove 'other religions' as false. But this is a complex topic, one that has been explored by the spiritually adept for millennia. It's not something that can be explained in a brief newspaper article.

So let's move away from the spiritual aspect of conversions and turn to material benefits. Undoubtedly, from this perspective, there can be both positive and negative results.

Besides the obvious efforts of faith-based groups in education and health, what can be the other material positives? What do you think will happen if we subject any group to competition, where they lose their own flock to others? Obviously, reforms! Efforts will be directed towards making themselves more attractive to their own followers, perhaps even to others. Let's elucidate this through the biggest present-day social problems in three religious groups: the caste system among Hindus, the child sex-abuse scandal among Christians, and extreme violence among Muslims. The victims of these social problems are primarily their own members. Those being oppressed by the perils of the caste system in Hinduism—a terrible corruption of ancient Vedic thought—are also Hindu. The tens of thousands of Western children (maybe hundreds of thousands, as some reports suggest) raped by Catholic priests, are Christian. Studies have proved beyond doubt that a vast majority suffering and dying from violence committed by radical Islamists and jihadists in the Arab world are Muslim.

Genetic research suggests that the rigid, birth-based caste system emerged less than 2,000 years ago, and it appeared very difficult to get rid of. But in the last seventy-odd years, Hindus have made dramatic improvements in this sphere, though I admit that there is a long way to go. What is the reason for this? There could be many, but it cannot be denied that one of the key factors driving current reforms is the fear of losing marginalized Hindus to other faiths. So competition has forced positive change.

The Roman Catholic Church simply denied the sex-abuse epidemic for many decades. But as the church started losing followers in record numbers in Europe and the US (primarily to atheists and the unaffiliated, but also to other faiths), they were forced to confront this problem. No less a person than Pope Francis admitted that there were many paedophiles among the Christian clergy. The first step towards solving a problem is accepting that there is one. I'm sure the church will work towards resolving this burning issue.

In most parts of the Arab world, religious conversion out of Islam is legally banned and punishable by death. So it is not possible for other faiths to offer competition. But if the Arabs open their hearts and minds to Islamic interpretations from liberal Muslims of India and Indonesia, and indeed to competition from other faiths, I'm sure they would significantly bring their problem of horrific violence under control.

Materially then, it appears as if religious conversions could offer some benefits. But these efforts are often accompanied by their own brand of problems. Conversions can also lead to resentment, unrest, social chaos and at times, even violence. In the Middle Ages, for instance, Europeans, Arabs, Mongols and Turks killed millions in the name of their faiths. How do we control this?

Like in any industry (and let's be honest, religious conversion is an industry now), there should be rules. First, funding for religious conversions should be scrutinized as per legal parameters and all the organizations that operate in India must file accounts in the country. Second, there should be parity, i.e., either every religious group should be legally allowed to proselytize without any opposition from the State/media/elite voices, or none should be allowed. Third, some troubling sources of funds and activities should be proscribed in India. For example, no peace-loving person would want Saudi Arabians to spread their version of Islam; most intelligence reports suggest that the Saudis fund and encourage religious violence, most of which is directed against those believed by the puritanical Saudis as 'impure Muslims'. (Having said that, it must be acknowledged that over the recent past, there have been massive liberal reforms in Saudi Arabia, with vastly improved women's rights and modernization efforts.) I think Indian Muslims, who are among the most pluralistic Muslims found anywhere, should be encouraged to spread their syncretic interpretations throughout the world. Some groups among the American evangelists should also be proscribed in India. Their version of Christianity is hate-filled and racist, quite unlike the peaceful version of Indian Christianity that we're familiar with. Visit www.joshuaproject.net to see the pernicious beliefs of these American evangelists, e.g., the 10/40 Window countries (between 10°N and 40°N; India is included) are called the 'Strongholds of Satan'. I can't imagine Indian Christians agreeing with this description of India. Lastly, obviously, any violence or calls to violence have to be strictly banned.

Once we place these controls, we should encourage all faiths to solicit conversions openly. We may benefit from it, at least materially.

Having said that, in my heart, I still feel that it's spiritually advisable to celebrate our own faith and also seek to reform, from within, any corruptions that have crept in; rather than wasting our time and our lives engaging in attempts to prove other religions wrong. For this will only lead us away from spiritual growth.

First published in *The Times of India,* March 2015

Religious Violence in India

I had just returned from an extended stay in the US on a fellowship programme and I must, at the outset, state that the Americans are, by and large, a very friendly and sociable people. The ones I met were also quite politically correct. Therefore, I was surprised by a question put forth by a concerned American: 'You may call it the "white man's burden", but have you considered that there might have been some positive outcomes of European colonial rule in India, such as preventing Hindus and Muslims from annihilating each other?' When confronted by my confounded look, the man asked: 'But aren't religious holocausts quite common in post-Independence India?'

That set me thinking. How did he get the impression that India is like Syria or Iraq? On closer examination, one couldn't blame him. He reads Western press reports on India, written by unmindful Western journalists—unmindful because most of them haven't learnt an Indian language or lived outside the bubble that anglicized-elite enclaves are in India. They frequently portray India as a communal tinderbox. These Western journalists build their opinions with help from our elite English-language media, a world in which secular as well as religious extremists have traditionally occupied a disproportionately loud voice: the former because they are insiders in this group and the latter because our English-language media loves controversial copy. Many of these secular-extremist journalists write searing articles on the 'massive' religious violence in India. Words like 'genocide', 'holocaust' and 'pogrom' are bandied about freely. The religious extremists, on the other hand, play up a sense of historical or communal hurt (depending on the religion of the target-group) and relentlessly call for retribution. Do these merchants of fear have a point?

The corporate world has a dictum: In God we trust; for everything else, show me data.

So I did some research. What do the numbers say about religious violence in India? Remember, this is not data about income-inequality among different religious groups, or religious discrimination leading to poverty. This data is on religious violence over the last fifty years.

Yes, we have had communal riots. There have been human tragedies, no doubt about it. We must crank up our administrative system to prevent these tragedies and deliver speedy justice when they do occur. We have had nearly sixty episodes of sectarian violence (incidents in which more than five people have been killed) in India since the mid-1960s, leading to a total death toll of over 13,000*. I repeat that they were terrible tragedies. In no manner will I belittle the suffering of the victims of religious killings. But were any of them holocausts, in which millions or even lakhs were killed? No. A holocaust is what Hitler carried out in Germany (six million deaths in the 1940s), what Churchill consciously precipitated in pre-Independence eastern India (1.5 to four million deaths in the 1940s), the Partition riots (one million deaths) or Pakistan's atrocities in East Pakistan, the nation we know as Bangladesh today (one to three million deaths in the 1970s). It is a fitting description of what is happening in Syria right now (1,60,000 to 4,00,000 deaths, and counting). Why, the Native American population was approximately ten million in North America when Columbus famously landed. It was reduced to less than a million by the time the genocide stopped.

Once again, without belittling the suffering of the victims of communal violence in India, we need to be careful with the words we use. Admittedly on an unrelated issue, according to the US CDC, in 2010 alone, there were over 30,000 gun-related deaths in the United States. That single year's gun-related death toll in the US is more than twice the total number of deaths in ALL the religious violence in India, cumulatively, in the last fifty years!

Now, I am not suggesting that everything is perfect in India. I am proud of my country, but pride should not blind us to our problems. There is indiscriminate killing taking place in India right now. But it's not due to communal strife. Over 5,00,000 female foetuses are illegally aborted annually in India, i.e., 5,00,000 girls are killed in the womb every year. This is 1,85,000 per cent more than the annual deaths in communal violence. Many more girl-children die from the systematic malnutrition that they are subjected to. Even when they grow up, Indian women suffer systemic harassment and violence. It's not just the government that oppresses them, but our entire society as a whole. If we want to save Indian lives, if we want to prevent a holocaust and gross injustice, this is where we need to focus. Across all religious/linguistic/caste/social segments, by far the most oppressed group in India today is women.

It seems that scare-mongering about religion suits our 'secular' and 'religious' extremists. I agree that religious strife is a problem; I would venture to add, it's a global problem that the human species is grappling with. But I seriously don't think India is going to sink into a morass of religious violence. While some of our communities may not live in perfect harmony with each other, we've learnt to coexist, by and large, without resorting to mass violence.

For all the fearful words that are used to describe religious people in India, a vast majority of Indians are like you and me: deeply religious, profoundly liberal and unwilling to die or kill for our faith. The numbers are clear proof of this. Sadly, we are not so non-violent when it comes to our girl-children and women. If we truly love the idea of India, we should focus on the issue of women's oppression, rather than attacking religion to assert our liberalism.

Sometimes, it's better to let the data speak, and desist from allowing fantastic prose to hog the limelight. You never know what agenda lies hidden beneath the prose.

First published in *Hindustan Times*, September 2014

Arguing Amicably

While in the US over a seven-week period in 2014, I found myself amazed by the animosity in their public debates. The so-called 'Left' and 'Right' commentators hold pre-decided positions on most issues. Their job: garner support for their camp, convinced as they are that theirs is the 'Absolute Truth' and the other side is 'Pure Evil' (yes, I did hear such phrases). They do not aim to find common ground. This debating style has, of late, stormed into the Indian media space. In an earlier era there was no public acrimony, because the Left dominated academic and communication platforms. Monopolies oftentimes drown out acrimony along with competition! The rise of the Right has energized debate; that's the good news. This *manthan* or churning of points-of-view will lead to the much-needed nuance. However, emulating the antagonistic American approach will derail the possibility of a common ground emerging.

I propose re-adoption of the principles of debate drawn from many ancient cultures (including our own), whose underlying premise was: no one can know the Absolute Truth. Modern science gave this esoteric idea a cool term: observer-bias, which professes that your values and expectations impact your perception of 'facts'. Even theoretical physicists factor it into their conclusions. Accepting this can instil humility, and thereby open the possibility of listening to an alternative point of view. If we approach even political events with the illumination of this prism-setting attitude, it leads to interesting insights. For example, judging by the opinions of journalists I've encountered, the Western media (*The New York Times*, *The Economist*, etc.) often sees itself as a force for Moral Good, readily pronouncing judgements and marketing 'universal values' to the world at large. However, the unfortunate Arabs in Iraq, Libya and Syria see them differently. Large sections of the Western media cheer-led the invasions/bombings of these ill-fated countries, which have led to the death of over one million Arabs. Yes, I underline, *over one million deaths*. An Arab friend remarked on the role of the Western media as, 'either colossally stupid or pure evil.' However, one cannot deny that Western media has also done some good, at least in their own societies. Perhaps if you accept the reality of the observer-bias, you may realize that the subtle truth, whatever it may be, lies somewhere in the much-ignored middle. Also, it's perhaps wise to be wary of the 'investigative skills' of Western media in non-Western countries.

The second suggestion is also based on the ancient worldview. Absolute Truth was elusive in all fields, except one: mathematics, also called the 'language of the universe'. In order to make arguments a little more 'truthful', use numbers to support your proposition. In other words: use data. Of late, India finds itself in the throes of a raging debate on rising intolerance, based on a few horrific incidents and some intemperate words. Every single life lost in violence, or in any other unnatural form, is tragic; but does the data reflect that religious violence is high or has ever been high in the last fifty years, compared to other forms of unnatural deaths in India? No. More women are killed in the womb EVERY fortnight, than the TOTAL number of people killed in ALL religious violence cumulatively in the last fifty years. Consider this: if we could stop female foeticide for just a fortnight, we would save more Indian lives than if we'd prevented every single religious riot/violent incident of the last fifty years. Some more data… More Indian children die of diarrhoea every forty-five days and more Indians are killed in road accidents every month than the TOTAL number killed in ALL acts of religious violence cumulatively in the last fifty years. Moreover, the numbers also reveal that religious violence has reduced considerably from its peak (the peak period of post-Independence religious violence extended from the 1960s to early 1990s). We know where our efforts, even our noise decibels, need to be directed. After all, data lends the correct perspective.

Lastly, I propose we approach serious issues with a calm mind. We should wait for investigations to be concluded before pronouncing judgements and conducting media trials. In the matter of the 'church-attack incidents' of early 2015, it later emerged that many of them didn't have any religious angle at all. Some were plain cases of robbery, one even attributed to the angst of a jilted non-Hindu lover. Also, at the time that four Delhi churches were vandalized, 200 temples, thirty gurudwaras and fifteen mosques were also vandalized. This suggests a state of general lawlessness rather than religious persecution. Even the Christian nun rape case of West Bengal (some in the media instantly held right-wing Hindus responsible) was actually perpetrated by illegal Bangladeshi-Muslim immigrants. Before someone imputes a Crusade–Jihad angle to this case, let me also clarify that investigations laid the blame on a money dispute. I am not suggesting that there are no religious fundamentalists or that there's no religious violence in India. But fortunately, the data reveals that relatively, when compared to our population size, it's in small numbers. India cannot be called communal. But it can certainly be called misogynistic. Or even uncaring towards hygiene or road-traffic rules.

If Indians who debate in the public square can accept observer-bias, foster the ability to listen, use data and most importantly, stay calm, we may just avoid the American spectacle where debates have degenerated to gladiatorial matches rather than an attempt to develop collective thought that is sophisticated, nuanced and productive.

First published in *The Times of India,* November 2015

Bane of Casteism

The tragic death of Rohith Vemula once again brought to the forefront the painful reality of caste discrimination in Indian society. Notwithstanding the noise generated by the relentless pursuit of politics, evidence clearly indicates that the Scheduled Castes (SC) as a group do face terrible prejudice in India.

Understandably, many non-westernized Indians would be loath to accept the 'atrocity literature' churned out by Western academics/NGOs. After all, among the most oppressed minorities in the civilized world are African-Americans and the European Romas, as evidenced by various detailed studies. However, the hypocrisy of Western academics/media/NGOs cannot be an excuse for Indians to not confront their own failings.

The present birth-based caste system and its attendant societal discrimination is a blot on India and completely at odds with conceptualizations of our ancient culture. There are some who claim that the present caste system is sanctified by our ancient scriptures. Not true.

Dr B.R. Ambedkar, in his scholarly book *Who Were the Shudras?*, used Indian scriptures and texts to prove that ancient India had powerful Shudra rulers as well, and the oppressive scriptural verses, justifying discrimination and a caste system based on birth, were interpolated into the texts much later. In the Bhagavad Gita, Lord Krishna clearly enunciates that He created the four varnas based on *guna* (attributes) and karma; birth is NOT mentioned. Rishis, or sages, were accorded the highest status in ancient India, and two of our greatest epics, the Ramayan and Mahabharat, were composed by Rishis who were not born of Brahmin parents. Valmikiji was the son of a Shudra and Krishna Dwaipayanaji (also known as Ved Vyas) was born to a fisherwoman. Satyakam Jabaliji, who is believed to have composed the celebrated *Jabali Upanishad*, was born to an unwed Shudra mother and his father's name was unknown. According to the Valmiki Ramayan, Jabaliji was an officiating priest and advisor to the Ayodhya royalty during Lord Ram's period. They all attained Brahminhood through their karma.

Arvind Sharma, professor of comparative religion at McGill University, states that caste rigidity and discrimination emerged in the Smriti period (from after the birth of Jesus Christ and extending up to 1200 CE) and was challenged in the medieval period by the Bhakti movement led by many non-upper caste saints. Powerful empires emerged that were led by Shudra rulers, e.g., the Kakatiyas. Later, the birth-based caste system became rigid once again around the British colonial period. It has remained so, ever since.

Scientific evidence provided by genetic research corroborates the ancient scriptural absence of a birth-based caste system. Banning of inter-marriage in pursuance of 'caste purity' is a fundamental marker of this birth-based caste system. Various scientific papers published in journals such as the *American Journal of Human Genetics*, *Nature* and *National Academy of Sciences Journal*, have established that interbreeding among different genetic groups in India was extremely common for thousands of years until it stopped around 0 CE to 400 CE (intriguingly, this is in sync with Arvind Sharma's suggested period when caste discrimination arose for the first time in recorded history). The inference might seem obvious. The present birth-based caste system—a distorted merger of *jati* (birth-community) and varna (personality and nature, based on guna and karma)—emerged approximately between 1,600–2,000 years ago. It did not exist earlier. Note that the word 'caste' itself is a Portuguese creation, derived from the Portuguese/Spanish, '*casta*' meaning breed or race.

The founding fathers of the Indian republic were, thankfully, aware of the pernicious effects of the birth-based caste system on Indian society. The Indian Constitution had bold objectives. But, as is obvious today, while government policies such as reservations have made a difference, it has not been good enough. The works of Dalit scholar Chandra Bhan Prasad show that the post-1991 economic reforms programme has seminally addressed this issue. According to the 2006–07 All-India MSME Census, approximately 14 per cent of the total enterprises in the country are owned by SC/ST entrepreneurs, and they generate nearly eight million jobs! The figure is probably much higher today.

There are many who claim that the reservations policy has ignored the upper caste poor and rural landless. This does hold some truth. But this is also largely due to the absence of adequate education facilities and jobs, which leads to rationing of the few opportunities that do exist. Post-1991 reforms have no doubt brought down shortfalls, but they have not gone far enough. Many argue that reformist policies will not only help Dalits, but also the rural and urban upper-caste poor.

So, as Chandra Bhan Prasad has pointed out repeatedly, more economic reforms and urbanization will go much further in mitigating caste discrimination and poverty in general, as compared to other government policies. However, regardless of the impact of economic reforms, caste discrimination must be actively opposed and fought against by all Indians; this must be done for the soul of our nation.

Annihilating the birth-based caste system is a battle we must all engage in at a societal level. We will honour our ancient culture with this fight. More importantly, we will end something that is just plain wrong.

First published in *The Times of India*, February 2016

Corruption Faultlines

Urban India is in the throes of obsessively examining the corrupt nature of polity and governance in our country. Anna Hazare's movement against corruption has galvanized our cities with a missionary zeal. Some zealous followers of Team Anna tell us that our nation's culture itself is corrupt. After all, don't we sell our precious votes for bottles of liquor from a person who must, preferably, also belong to our 'community'? Isn't nepotism the norm, and not the exception? Why, we even attempt to bribe God with offerings in exchange for blessings! The verdict is clear, it would seem: we are an inherently corrupt people with little hope of change but for a massive revolution.

But hold on a moment. Are we really a corrupt nation? Is being amoral intrinsic to the nature of an Indian citizen?

India, as is widely acknowledged, is an ancient civilization but a young nation. For large parts of our civilizational life, and certainly so in the last millennia, we have been an agrarian conglomeration with a few pockets of periodic urban efflorescence. Even the post-Independence reality of India has been predominantly rural. On the other hand, the Western world urbanized a few centuries before us.

The moral order in an agrarian society differs from the urban. The former is governed on kinship, loyalty and honour-based codes that are essentially the law of the community. Justice lies in the collective honour and prestige of your clan, comprising the family, caste, tribe … in its essence, the *biradari*. You stand by your own. You will compromise the interests of abstract institutions for the sake of your people.

You will perjure yourself in court on behalf of your relatives; but you will refrain from doing so in a panchayat, where everyone knows everyone else and lying, in any case, is pointless. Falsehood prevails in our lower courts of justice. Not because we are amoral, but because those who lie in courts, do not feel they are doing anything wrong. Quite the contrary, they are in fact being true to the higher moral law of loyalty to their clan. Even in the cities, many do all they can, in keeping with their status, contacts and resources, to deceive, pressure, influence and bribe the police and the courts in the interests of their relatives and associates. They convince themselves that it is the right thing to do; it is, truth be told, for it is an alternative code of conduct.

Many have helped their 'own' get jobs in organizations, though these dear ones may not have been the most deserving and therefore not ideal for the organization. The ill-paid bureaucrat will accept bribes so he can fulfil the role of a good son, brother or father. The ancient ethics of loyalty to your own outweighs laws that are designed by an abstract society in the making.

Justice in agrarian societies is restorative. Sending the perpetrators of a crime to jail is an urban practice. Clan justice aims at compromise, compensation and negotiation. It usually becomes punitive only in extreme circumstances.

It is routine these days to malign our politicians and dismiss them as reprehensible. Keep in mind, though, that India is probably the first country in the world that democratized before it urbanized/modernized. In truth, we are still primarily a rural country; many 'citizens' even in our cities possess the impulses and moral code of a tribal society.

Our savvy politicians emerge and survive in this ecosystem. They are not elected by an abstract agglomeration of 'citizens', but by 'their own'—and 'their own' people legitimately expect to be looked after. I know of a politician whose entire village turned up on his manicured lawn in Mumbai for his birthday, all ten thousand of them. They expected to be adequately fed and feted. How is the politician supposed to drum up the funds to do so? Patronage survives because the masses view it as appropriate. It is hypocritical for intellectual elites to want democracy on the one hand, and on the other, expect politicians to be blind to the expectations of the masses who vote them to power; instead, self-appointed societal pundits want politicians to only find direction from them. No doubt, some politicians single-mindedly pursue personal gain and self-aggrandizement; it is so in all human societies; put it down to human nature. But there are many other politicians who do not. The flow of money is primarily geared towards winning, retaining and rewarding supporters; and towards providing assistance to kinship groups. The situation is exacerbated by the absence of realistic and pragmatic ways in which political parties and politicians can raise legitimate funds.

On the other hand, an urban society is conceptually based on abstract laws and formal institutions. It aims to generate alternative loyalties, along with a different code of ethics that transcends kinship commitments. Not because this is a superior way to be. It is only a different way in which a society can organize itself when ancient tribal bonds get eclipsed in the anonymity of urban life. Optimizing self-interest is an important underlying motive behind any human organization. New social structures evolve and replace the earlier when people begin to view them as serving their selfish interest, more efficiently.

This need first expresses itself in communities of small immigrant groups. Willy-nilly, they find themselves distanced from their traditional codes of conduct, and over a period of time grow to appreciate, even validate, state-driven structures of administration. We are at that stage in our evolution as a democracy. We have one foot firmly planted in ancient kinship culture; of which we are justifiably the proud inheritors, no doubt. The other foot, though, is extending towards the modern world. We live in times of furious redefinitions—integrity too is being redefined. Were we genetically corrupt in the past? No. Are we genetically corrupt today? No. We are simply realigning our goal posts in times of change. Remaining true to character, this must happen softly and non-violently in this land of the Mahatma.

So in this New Year, I will state once again: there are many faults in my land. And we have a long way to go. But I'm still damn proud to be Indian!

First published in *The Asian Age/Deccan Chronicle,* 2011

Representative Government and the Will of the People

I try to follow a golden rule in my columns and interviews: avoid speaking or writing on politics. There are many reasons for this. One of them is that I like to reflect upon topics before I write on them. Therefore, usually, by the time I arrive at an opinion on a political event, it is not topical anymore. In June 2014, when this article was commissioned by a newspaper, an issue had arisen in our country's political theatre that I had thought about even in the past. Therefore, I decided to present my views on the subject.

Some establishment intellectuals had been making a point as follows: in the then general elections, since the National Democratic Alliance or NDA had garnered 38.5 per cent of the vote (and BJP 31 per cent), their victory was somehow incomplete/illegitimate. We were told that 61.5 per cent of Indians had rejected the NDA (and 69 per cent had rejected the BJP) and therefore it wasn't a truly representative government. Was that fair criticism? I examined the issue in the larger perspective.

Let's step back a bit. Why does a government exist? Is it to primarily represent the country as a mini-embodiment of the diverse cultures, peoples and viewpoints of the nation? Or does it exist in order to govern?

The Greek philosopher Plato clearly believed that the government's primary purpose was to take charge and govern a society. In fact, he held democracy in disdain. The best form of government, for him, was theocracy—divine rule—which he postulated was impossible in practical terms. Plato's second preference was aristocracy: a rule of philosopher-kings, or as he called them, men-of-silver. These were visualized as men who were systematically trained to be better than the people they led, so that they could guide the spiritual and material development of their country.

Ancient Indians also held that the primary task of a government was to govern and not represent its country's diverse viewpoints. But they believed that monarchs should not be allowed to exercise absolute power; which is why raj gurus (royal preceptors) and rajya sabhas (or royal councils) existed in ancient India, in order to exert some measure of control on rulers. However, even these controls were not instituted with the intent to coerce the monarchs into 'representing the views of the people'. They were put in place to ensure that the monarch followed Raj Dharma or royal duties.

There were 'democracies-of-sorts' in the ancient world which did give space to the views of some others, besides the rulers, e.g., the famous Vajji Sangha* in India or the governments of ancient Athens. But even in these instances, the so-called 'representation' was not for the common people, but the elite. In ancient Athens, for example, slaves and women were not allowed to vote.

The highpoint of democracy has been the modern age. In democracies today, universal adult suffrage is, well, universal. Even so, practically all voting systems have been designed such that primacy is given to governance over representation of the various points of view of all the peoples of the country. And since governance is given precedence, almost all election systems have been designed such that higher voting patterns lead to a disproportionately higher share in the legislature or elected executive of the country. Why? Because stability is a prerequisite for governance. If one tries to form a government where every single viewpoint is to be represented, then one is planning for endless paralysis and ultimately, chaos.

Therefore, the US has electoral colleges for presidential elections, wherein a voting majority is exaggerated into a much larger electoral college majority (the US President is technically elected by the Electoral College and not directly by the people; the people only elect the Electoral College). This has led, in four cases, to Presidents being elected despite a minority in direct voting percentage. And some of those Presidents proved to be competent, even remarkable.

In proportional voting, a recent favourite with the Indian establishment intellectuals, normally there is a cut-off below which a party gets no seats in the legislature. In Germany, for example, the cut-off used to be 5 per cent (Germany also has a direct election system for a few seats; a court ruling had made some further changes in proportional representation, but I will ignore that for now in the interest of simplicity). Had we followed a proportional voting system in India with a cut-off, all regional parties and independents would have got no seats in the 2014 elections, as their national voting percentage was less than 5 per cent. Only the BJP and Congress would have got seats in the Lok Sabha. The election results, under proportional representation with a cut-off, would roughly have been the same for the BJP/NDA, if not better. However, the regional parties would have been wiped out and their seats would have gone to the Congress.

The sum and substance is that every election system (be it the US electoral college, proportional representation or our own first-past-the-post) has been deliberately designed to encourage stability and governance while also bringing in some adequate measure of representation of the views of the people.

So to all those who complained that in the general elections of 2014, a minority lead in voting percentage had been disproportionately converted into a majority in parliamentary seats: well, yes, that is the way the system has been designed. That is the way that ALL electoral systems across the world have been designed. Because the purpose of any election system is not to create a mini-embodiment of the views of every single person in the country. The purpose of an election is to elect a government that is capable of governing.

Of course, my views should not be construed as being either supportive of or opposing any political formation. They're meant to address the concerns of those who would seek to interpret the results of a major election in a certain narrow way and question our electoral system itself. I am simply defending the system, not any political party. And to those who were unhappy with the 2014 election results, and continue to negate it, I say: be mature, respect the people's mandate. And if you didn't like the election results, come back and campaign harder in the next election. That is the essence of democracy.

Additional Point

I think the recent Brexit result in the UK would certainly give pause for thought to all those who aggressively argued against the legitimacy of the electoral results of May 2014. Democracy is not an excuse for leaders to leave complex decision-making to the people and force them to make binary choices based on emotions and personal experiences. Democracy is a system that gives the common people a voice that cannot be ignored and a feeling of ownership of their government. But the decisions have to be taken by the government, which will be judged on its performance on an overall basis, at the next election. Complex decisions should not be delegated to the people through referendums; as Clement Atlee said, referendums are a 'device for dictators and demagogues'. It is intriguing that many of those who questioned the legitimacy of the Indian government elected in 2014, given that a majority of voters did not vote for the government, are now questioning the Brexit result despite a *majority* of people in the UK having voted for it. Clearly, the founding fathers of many democracies designed most electoral systems with balances, with the intention to elect a government capable of governing; and they were far wiser than our present-day establishment intellectuals. Once again, I am not supporting or opposing any political formation in India. I am simply extolling the wisdom of a system which gives people a voice in the government, but balances it with the needs of stability and governance. As our President had said, there is a difference between democracy and mobocracy.

First published *in Hindustan Times,* June 2014

One Thing at a Time

During my days as a hard-working competitor in the corporate rat-race, I was fond of a homily. It would be displayed prominently wherever I worked, right from my cubicle days to the time when I moved into a rather nice cabin: 'Life is short, the road is long. Hurry…'

I loved that statement. It exemplified my attitude towards my career, in fact my life. Needless to say, I expected everyone in my team to share that attitude; I even tried to enforce it on my bosses, the cheek of it all! My constant refrain was: we have little time in this one life. We should embrace every challenge that comes our way; pack in as much as we can into our day, make it count. Carpe diem! Seize the day! What a kick-ass attitude, right? You can almost visualize an American motivational speaker screaming these words at you, even as you read.

Looking back, I'm amazed at how immature and facile I was. I had packed my life with, quite frankly, futile endeavours; pursuits which added no value to my life or to which I added no value in return. Today, I have re-learnt the wisdom that was taught to me as a child; one that I had lost track of in my efforts at being a spunky corporate warrior. We are Indians. Our cultural meme accommodates the concept of multiple lives; can there really be such a thing as shortage of time? When you realize that you don't have to experience everything in this one life, then you can prioritize. I am working harder now than I did in my corporate avatar. But I'm certainly not as perennially exhausted as I used to be; because I prioritize. I only do what I consider important at that moment in time. I don't take on things that I do not want to do, simply because I don't feel I need to prove anything to myself anymore. For example, I used to party extensively because I felt pressured by relationships. Now I only socialize when I want to. In the past, I would take on additional projects even if I was snowed under with work—it would always seem unavoidable. Today, if I don't have the time, I simply refuse; because I know that the opportunity will return, either in this life or the next!

Accepting that we live multiple lives gives us so much clarity; it takes the pressure off and helps us get centred and grounded. We can then focus on what truly matters. So what do I focus on? Writing my books, propagating our culture/philosophies, spending time with my family, travelling, listening to music and reading. That's it. All other things get attention only if I have spare time. Remember, when it comes to unimportant projects, one can simply say, I'll leave this for my next life!

First published in *India Today*, 2015

The Age of Money

Imagine you're a fierce Mongol/Turkic warrior in the Middle Ages, a proud soldier in one of the most fearsome armies ever. Your conquering horde has brought death and devastation to China, Arabia, Europe and India. You see yourself as the finest specimen of a warrior. Let us now imagine that, through the miracle of science, you time-travelled into the twenty-first century. Would you be surprised by what you saw in terms of social structure? Certainly!

The best lifestyle today is available not to heads of state (the equivalent of kings of the soldier's era) or even army chiefs. Instead, it is the privilege of successful businessmen. An army general earns less than a mid-level employee in a multinational corporation. Businessmen actually make *demands* upon their political leaders, unlike in the time-travelling soldier's days when, aware of their inferior status, they approached kings as supplicants. Most modern youth undergo training to join companies or start businesses, unlike in the Middle Ages when the meritorious would aspire to join the army. This may surprise the time-travelling soldier, but not us. Why?

Because we live in the Age of Money, or as our texts state, the Age of Vaishya. This does not refer to the caste, but the caste-*profession*. Therefore, the Age of Brahmin is the Age of Knowledge; the Age of Kshatriya is the Age of Warrior Skills and Militarism; and the Age of Shudra is the Age of Individualism. These ages keep recurring in an endless cycle of time. In the Age of Kshatriya, those who are proficient in warfare and violence are powerful and respected; the ones who create wealth and money through trade and business will be so in the Age of Vaishya. Importantly, the most efficient means of effecting societal change rests upon the dominant caste-profession of the age that you live in.

Let me attempt to explain this construct with the help of the Age of Militarism (which we've recently emerged from) and the Age of Money (which we live in today).

In the Age of Militarism, the most important currency of change was violence. Religions were propagated and defended with violence—most major religions that have survived to this day were defended in the Middle Ages by able and iconic warriors, like Saladin and Richard the Lionheart. The most effective way for people to raise their status was through militant might; it is no surprise then, that the army was a revered institution, across most cultures. Today we see that nations that are excessively violent do not prosper, e.g., Somalia. But in the Age of Militarism, people who were adept at violence became pre-eminent in the world, e.g., the Mongol/Turkic tribes. Money or knowledge was not the most efficient route to power in the Age of Militarism. The art of making money or practicing knowledge did exist, but it was not the dominant currency of change. The successful leader was not the one who was surrounded by a tribe of rich or educated people (though they had their uses), but one who was accompanied by the most fearless warriors.

Today, we live in the Age of Money, or the way of the Vaishya. The most efficient currency of change is money, and not violence. Some accept the rules of the age and prosper; others don't and suffer.

Has India made a shift from the Age of Militarism to the Age of Money? I think we're in a muddle. We have left the Age of Militarism behind, thanks largely to one of the greatest leaders of the last century, Mahatma Gandhi. We Indians have created an illusion for ourselves that we were always a non-violent people. That's not true. We've had our share of violent adventurism, e.g., the brutal Pala–Chola wars. Mahatma Gandhi's influence (building on parts of our ancient philosophical heritage) dramatically reduced the attraction for violence among most Indians, thus pulling us out of the Age of Kshatriya.

But have we entered the Age of Vaishya wholeheartedly? Not quite. We have a complicated relationship with money. Many, especially from our older generation, who occupy positions of power, are of the view that money leads to corruption. We have a Brahminical/Kshatriya disdain for money (although our youth suffer less from this attitude). This exhibits itself in the way we conduct our lives, our relationships, even in the obscene extravagance of our wealthy class, which is a symptom of an unhealthy relationship with money.

Can money damage society and cause harm, sometimes? Definitely. But then, so did violence in the Age of Kshatriya, knowledge in the Age of Brahmin, or individualism in the Age of Shudra. It is not money itself that is the problem, but our attitude to it.

In the Age of Militarism, there were dharmic warriors like the Samurai of Japan, who fought with a warrior code (the Bushido code). They believed that they had a mission, incorporated within which was protection of the weak. But there also were *adharmic* warriors, who used their skill to torment the innocent and weak. Similarly, today, there are dharmic moneymakers and *adharmic* moneymakers.

What should common Indians do in this Age of Money? Firstly, we should shed our hypocrisy about money and accept the rules of this age. Those who preach that money is corrupting and capitalism is evil, are being as irresponsible as those who preached non-violence in the Age of Militarism. Secondly, we should celebrate our dharmic moneymakers, like societies in the Age of Militarism celebrated their great warriors. Thirdly, we must accept that knowledge, violence and individualism also have relevance in our age, but they cannot be used as efficiently as money, in effecting change. Pakistan is attempting to change its global status by using violence above all other means, while China has primarily used money as a tool for transformation. Which nation is more successful? Can that even be a serious question? Lastly, we must understand that even when knowledge is used today, its likelihood of success is further enhanced when supported by money, e.g., even thinkers and intellectuals are largely ignored unless they're well marketed.

And what should an aspiring moneymaker do? Be dharmic and earn money the right way, without breaking laws; spend wisely; control indulgences and flamboyant urges; contribute towards charity and help the underprivileged. This will earn good karma and give you happiness beyond what money can buy.

We live in the Age of Money. Maybe the Age of Knowledge or Militarism or Individualism will follow; it might most likely be the Age of Individualism. But today, we should understand the rules of our age. With apologies to Deng Xiaoping for twisting his words ever so slightly, our country's slogan needs to be: To earn money is glorious!

First published in *Hindustan Times,* 2013

The Ancient Indian Approach to Charity and Inclusiveness

I've been invited here to speak on the topic of charity and inclusiveness. Before I begin, I'd like to ask a few as to why you think inclusiveness is important. I believe the subject has been discussed already in other sessions today, right? So why do you think inclusiveness is important?

Response from the audience:

All sections of society come together.

That's a nice thought. And I agree with you.

Stability.

Yes. It's in our own enlightened, selfish interest that there's inclusiveness in our society. For it ensures stability. Economies need fast growth to become rich, but, normally, inequality also rises in them simultaneously. Let me give you the example of South American countries. It's difficult to imagine today, but the countries of South America were once viewed the way East Asian countries like South Korea are viewed, today. South Korea is now part of the developed world; in fact it will be richer than most countries of Europe soon. Around fifty years ago, Argentina and Brazil were also viewed similarly. Where is Argentina today? That's one of the practical problems with inequality, besides, of course, its moral dimension. Inequality beyond an acceptable limit leads to divisive and confrontational politics. Which is what happened in many South American countries like Argentina. This can end up destroying society itself, and eventually hurt even those who are doing well economically. It is therefore in the enlightened, selfish interest of even the rich that there isn't too much inequality in society.

However, some inequality is a given in all human societies. In fact, in nature itself. That is the reality of life. No society is ever exactly equal. But inequality must be managed, so that it is never excessive. Everyone must have a fair chance at success, after which it's up to them what they make of their lives.

Now, one current paradigm to handle inequality is—for want of a better term—the Western paradigm. How does this work? Simply put, you guilt-trip the rich. This is one part of the paradigm. For example, most of you in this room would be among the better off people in India and the Western paradigm idea is to guilt-trip you; you *must* do charity, because it's your duty, almost your atonement for being successful. The second part of this model is for the rich to have intermediaries. It could be an NGO or some other institution; often multinational NGOs and institutions. The third leg of this paradigm comprises the recipients of this charity. The philosophical message to these recipients is that receiving this charity is their right; no one is doing them a favour.

This modern paradigm for inclusiveness has its benefits. But there are also some downsides. There are large numbers of interesting reports from a few NGOs themselves, in places like Africa, where many recipients have become charity addicts. They get used to receiving charity and do not feel the need to be productive citizens and raise themselves above poverty. And if the charity stops, they get agitated and angry. Sometimes it leads to social chaos. The donors too face a moral challenge. Often, not always but very often, they do charity to assuage themselves in the public domain. They choose charity formats that are PR-*able*, that help them manage their public image with suitable effect. *Charity karo aur photo newspaper mein chhaapo* (Do charity and get a picture in a newspaper). One fallout of this is that charity may be directed towards PR-*able* causes and not those which the society may actually need.

The third dimension, of course, is the NGO industry. Oftentimes these NGOs don't really help the society. Take the mining industry; I won't name the company, but a mining company was blocked from mining in an Indian state due to local protests. It emerged later that one of the NGOs which had led the agitation was funded by a mining company in the US with vested interests! This is business competition managed in the garb of charity. This is the Western paradigm of charity.

I'd like to present you with another paradigm, one that I will call the Indian paradigm of charity; or more correctly, the *ancient* Indian paradigm of charity. There are two dominant approaches to charity in India which hark back to ancient philosophical ideas: one is the Indic approach—the Hindu, Buddhist, Jain and Sikh approach—and the other is the Indian Islamic approach.

In the Indic approach, it is believed that the *recipient* of the charity is actually *doing a favour* to the *person who gives charity*. How so? This is based on the logic of karma. You know the logic of karma, right? That we carry the weight of our own karma, that all the good or bad deeds we do impact us in this life or the next. If you want to know what your past karma was like, then examine your current life, because it's a consequence of your past karma. And if you want to know what your future will be like, then examine your karma today. You are creating your future right now. So, the belief is that the recipient of your charity is doing you a good turn because he's taking a debt in his own karma account for your sake, which he will need to pay back sometime, either in this life or the next. And the giver of charity is balancing his karma account; he is repaying some debt. So, in the Indic approach, the *giver of charity* is the actual beneficiary of an act of charity.

The Indian Islamic way has the concept of *zakat*. Are there any Indian Muslims among you? You guys know the concept of *zakat*, right? My Bohri Muslim friends have told me about it; a percentage of their income is given to charity. You can either do it directly or through an institution. And this is your duty to God; you are not doing anyone a favour.

The Indian approach has been practiced in the country for centuries before the British arrived. What are the benefits of this as compared to the Western paradigm? Imagine the impact on the recipient of the charity, the person who is receiving it. I'd like to relate a personal story about my family. I come from a humble background. My family was middle class, and middle class of the India of the 1970s was very different from the middle class of today. In the '70s and '80s, which is when I was growing up, if you were able to feed your family and send your children to school, you were middle class. A generation earlier, my grandfather was a man of very limited means. Being from a very humble background, he didn't have the money to educate himself well. How many of you have heard of Pandit Madan Mohan Malaviya? Awesome, delighted that you have.

He was the founder of Benaras Hindu University (BHU). He mentored a charity programme through which he funded the education of talented children of limited means. One of the children who benefitted from this charity was my grandfather. He was a very poor but a very smart boy and because of Madan Mohan Malaviyaji's munificence, he rose dramatically in life. He became a teacher, he also became a pandit in Kashi. He had eight children; families were super large those days. So today, there are at least seventy people who have descended from my grandfather and for all of us—our lives, our future, was shaped dramatically by Pandit Malaviyaji's charity. What do you think is my family's attitude toward that charity which our ancestor, one poor boy in Kashi, received all those decades ago? Do we think it was our right to receive that charity? Most certainly not. It's quite the contrary—the conscious responsibility that that gesture of Pandit Malaviyaji generated, infuses my extended family's character to this day. We have taken on a debt, a karmic debt, and it is our duty to repay that debt by carrying that gesture forward; or else the karmic burden would weigh down our souls. Malaviyaji, wherever he is, might not even know of our existence. And it's not just my grandfather's life he transformed; there were countless others. And he didn't seek anything in return from us. Imagine the effect this had, or should have had, on my family. We know that we have taken a debt on our familial soul; we must pass it on. How do we pass it on? By doing charity. Which means that, firstly, we have to ensure that we earn enough to be able to do charity. If all the recipients of charity were to have this attitude, it would provide the psychological impetus to pull them out of poverty. Ultimately, the only person who can propel you upwards in life is you yourself. No one, not even God, can help those who do not want to help themselves.

This is the philosophical difference in attitude when the recipient believes that he is held accountable by the laws of karma for having received charity from someone else. The donor is also impacted by this alternative philosophy. Instead of basking in egotistical and self-gratifying glory for having 'done good'; he has a humbling sense of cleansing his karma through his action; that the person who has received his charity has done him a favour. Not for a moment will he be thinking about the PR*ability* of his charitable act. There's a strong possibility that he might not stop at simply writing a cheque, but offer something far more valuable: his time and his expertise, if only to make sure that the job is well done; that it actually helps someone, impacts someone's life positively.

Also, imagine the impact on the intermediaries. The ancient Indian way was to think local. If those who are conducting the work have little or no idea about the local, cultural and environmental peculiarities, it can result in a phenomenal waste of effort and money. In traditional India, much of the conduits for charity were temples. How many Punjabis here? Good North Indian contingent! You have the concept of *langar* in Punjab, right? The gurudwara feeds all those who visit; it's magnificent charity and the seva is performed by all, from the humblest to the high and mighty. This practice was prevalent in all temples, across India, till a few centuries ago. What is called *prasad* today, was actually the feeding of the poor. Food was offered to all who came. Ancient temples in India were also the institutions of education, which was also local. Training in local skills was offered, and it would be put to use locally. Sadly, since British times (and the policy continued post-Independence), the government has taken over most temples in India. And we all know what happens when the government takes over something. So when temples were taken over in this fashion, with decision-makers sitting in capital cities far away, many of these functions performed by temples ceased to operate. It's beneficial when the charity-giver and the beneficiaries are local. They actually know what works in that area. They are not strangers who have descended with a 'saviour complex'; people who are clueless about what the locals want or need.

This is our own model of charity and inclusiveness. It may work better in our own country as compared to the Western model that we have currently imported. If we can actually put some thought into our concept of charity, we can finally pay heed to the wise Vidur from the Mahabharat. He said that there are two ways to waste money. One is by giving money or charity to the unworthy. And the other is by *not* giving it to the worthy. Learn from Vidur; make sure you do charity and make sure that your charity is put to good use. There's a wealth of wisdom in the traditional Indian way; we can choose to tap into it and lead better lives today.

Franklin Templeton Conference on Inclusive Prosperity, February 2016

The Voice of the Religious Liberals

Q: Amish, this was really one of the best sessions which I heard since yesterday. This was absolutely fantastic. My question to you is, are you a Sri Aurobindoite? Have you read Sri Aurobindo?

A: I have read some works of Sri Aurobindo. Regrettably, I must say I haven't spent as much time in Auroville as I would have liked to. Fortunately, I am not a banker anymore, so I have a little more time to do things that I like. I do intend to spend time in Auroville. Someday soon I'll visit Pondicherry (Puducherry).

Q: Yes, all that you said seems to reflect Sri Aurobindo. So it was good.

A: Thank you, thank you so much.

Q: Organized religion is no different from organized crime. True or false?

A: I would disagree. I am a Hindu and our religion is more decentralized and does not fit the description of 'organized religion'. But organized religion plays its own role. The point is, many philosophies depend on the people driving them, for their understanding. Organized religions have created a lot of good as well and I can give you many examples to prove my point. Buddhism, as it was taught by Gautam Buddha and the original Sangha. Christianity, as it was practiced by Jesus Christ. Jesus preached the simple message of love at a time of historical violence and conquest by the Roman empire. He suggested that one can choose one's community in times that were feudal. It was inspirational and revolutionary. Organized religion can be a force for good, of course. But just like all other things, a few bad men can misuse religion as well. It has happened everywhere—in our country too. The task that confronts us religious liberals is to speak up loudly. If we don't, we allow religious extremists and secular extremists, who in my opinion are both misguided, to snatch the narrative away from us; we allow them to insult our religions with their extremism.

Q: Have you faced anger from people because the subject you write about involves Gods. People are really touchy about Gods and mythical figures. Has anyone come up to you and said how dare you write like this about Gods?

A: Not at all. Honestly, there is no better country than India for an author like me. I'm not being facetious or politically correct; I mean it when I say this. Look at our past. We have a rich tradition of modernizing and localizing our myths that extends over millennia. There are various versions of the Ramayan. The version that is most popular in north India today is the Ramcharitmanas, which is actually a sixteenth-century modernization of the original Valmiki Ramayan. In the Valmiki Ramayan, for example, Sitaji is a much stronger character. There's a version of the Ramayan called the *Adbhut Ramayan* in which Sitaji kills the elder Raavan. I should clarify that there are two Raavans in that version. And the main Raavan is the elder one. The Ramayan of the tribal areas of Jharkhand and Chhattisgarh envisions Sitaji as a warrior. Although the *Kamba Ramayanam* from Tamil Nadu reveres Lord Ram, both as a God as well as the hero of the epic, it also extols the virtues of Raavan. Let us shift our attention to the Puranas. The myths about creation from the *Shiva Purana*, the *Vishnu Purana* and the *Brahma Purana* are equally compelling, though pointedly different. Historians tell us that the *Brahma Purana* is probably 2,000–2,500 years old. I believe that it is 4,500–5,000 years old, but let's concede that point to the historians for the moment. Maybe it's 2,000 years old; but the *Brahma Purana* mentions the Konark temple which we all know was built 800 years ago. So what does that indicate? The *Brahma Purana* that we read today was perhaps edited 800 years ago. The point I am trying to make is that this tradition of modernizing and localizing myths has been an ongoing process because in India, religiosity and liberalism always went hand in hand. We merely lost touch with this heritage in the last few centuries. I am not doing anything that is *less* Indian. I am actually being *more* Indian by charting my own path to God. That is why I'm not surprised that there's been no controversy. By God's grace, my books are not a secret any more. I haven't faced any protests or anything of the sort.

Q: You are a brilliant author, but do you realize you have created a little storm in many Indian homes? Young kids come to parents and say that they told them a different story about Shiva and Parvati and here is this man who tells them a story which they believe. Are you planning to rewrite Indian mythology and is the Shiva Trilogy just a starting point and are there many more to come? Can you describe the newer things you are planning to do? I mean it seems like you are rewriting Indian mythology.

A: No, I won't lay claim to such a big task of rewriting Indian mythology. I am only doing what comes naturally to me. I've been blessed by Lord Shiva with this story. And I have been blessed with many other stories that are interconnected to the Shiva Trilogy. I will write all of them over the next two or three decades. Having said that, I do want to state that there has always been a rich tradition of questioning in India. At our core, through most of our history, we have been a freedom-loving, passionate, rebellious—frankly even a slightly insolent people. We may have forgotten this aspect of our culture a few centuries ago, but today, I believe, we are rediscovering it. Lord Krishna gives us a clear message in the eighteenth *adhyay* (chapter) of the Bhagavad Gita. The Gita is an allegorical message. Lord Krishna is not just talking to Arjun; He speaks to all of us. And He says, 'I have given you knowledge most profound. Now your task is to think deeply about it and do what you think is right.' Essentially He's asking us to use our own mind, for it's been given to us for a purpose. We must question; it is, in fact, our duty. So if the youth are questioning things, it's good. Preferably, it should be done politely. There's no need to get into scraps with parents or others but there's nothing wrong with questioning. It's our culture, our ancient way.

Q: You know what I am really amazed by, more than even your books, is actually your retention power. You are able to quote from all sorts of different sources and I wonder where that comes from because we live in such a fast-paced world that you even forget the content of the last text you sent. You can't remember anything. So what are you doing? Are you taking memory tablets? Are you reading a lot? I'm actually curious to know this.

A: Okay, I love reading and I eat a lot of badaam! I've been told it's good for memory. But seriously, I read a lot. Also, I grew up in a very religious household. It was the good fortune of my birth. My grandfather, Pandit Babulal Tripathi, was a professor at BHU. My parents are deeply religious and quite simply, we learnt a lot of our scriptures right at home. Also, we were not taught that one religion is better than the other or that you are not supposed to question. My grandfather used to say that if you question, then you understand things more deeply and if you understand things more deeply, then they get embedded in the deep recesses of your mind. The essential point of questioning is to understand. For instance, the meaning of the word 'upanishad' itself is to sit at the feet of a guru, and then, ask questions. You can never remember things for long if you learn them by rote. But if you understand, then they get burnt into your consciousness, and you seldom forget.

Q: In *The Oath of the Vayuputras*, you talk about Vishnu and Shiva and good and evil and you just now also said Shiva lives around us. I have a question which is probably more profound. Doesn't Shiva live within us?

A: That was actually the point of my speech, sir. Lord Shiva lives within us and that is the concept of advait. In fact it is an idea that exists across all religions. In the *Book of Luke* from the Holy Bible, we are told very clearly, 'Behold the kingdom of God is among you.' Across all religions, this Advaitic idea of non-duality, of unity, conveys the message that God exists in everything; not just within us humans, but everything in nature: in the trees, the sea, the stars, the rivers, all creatures … everywhere.

Q: I'm a Shiva bhakt as well and my son is called Shiv but what I want to ask you is—somehow you know about so many religions, but Shivji seems to be above everybody and everything. For instance, if somebody wrote about Ram smoking a chillum or something, people would probably really object and there would be a big hue and cry, but Shivji seems to just get away with it and get away with everything because he is sort of above everything. What do you have to say about that?

A: Firstly, yes, even in His traditional forms, Lord Shiva is a very cool God; no doubt about that. And I mean no disrespect to any other God. One of my younger readers had written to me saying Lord Shiva is the Dude of the Gods. He is actually the God of the rebels. I am slightly rebellious by nature and for people like me, He is a very attractive God. Why? He's very democratic. He does not talk down to His devotees. He is respectful and loving towards His wife. He's a dazzling dancer, a brilliant musician, a fierce warrior, and an intellectual; He's the source of the Vedas and as you pointed out, yes, He does drink bhang as well. He's a fun God to write about. But I want to say one more thing; I'm frequently asked a question, 'Do I think that Lord Shiva is the supreme God?' I always fall back on this lovely line from the *Rig Veda*: Truth is one but the wise men speak it as many. God is one but He can be approached in many different ways. God can approach us in many different forms. He can come to us as Lord Vishnu, He can come to us as Shakti Maa, He can come to us as Jesus Christ, He can come to us as Allah, He can come to us through Gautam Buddha, He can come to us through Mahavir, He can come to us through Guru Nanak. He comes to us in different forms because we are different people. The rebel in me was attracted to Lord Shiva. Others may appreciate a different form of God because we are all different. But they are all part of the same source. No God is higher or lower. God, in fact, is the truth. Let me tell you another story, one that I heard in Ajmer Sharif. Whenever we are in Jaipur and we have some time, my wife and I like to take a detour to Ajmer Sharif. On one of our trips, we met a maulvi and he told me a story from the life of Shams and Rumi. Apparently Shams said to Rumi: one day, a man died in the early hours of a morning. His soul was released from the fetters of his body and it began to fly. Higher and higher it soared, beyond the city, the earth, very soon it was beyond the solar system. It flew higher, beyond the Milky Way galaxy, beyond the universe, beyond the multiple universes that exist till it reached the source of the source of light. It found God and it said, 'My Lord, there is this tiny, small, insignificant little planet far, far away called earth. Does it matter to you as to what religion they follow out there; the version of God they worship?' God answered, 'It doesn't; follow whichever path your heart resonates with, they all lead to me.' The maulvi's eyes were brimming with tears as he finished his story. This is the essence of spirituality in India.

India Today Conclave, March 2013

A Guarantor of Liberalism

An unfortunate trope among the global liberal elite is the demonization of patriotism. Often, some extremist nationalist groups of the twentieth century, such as the Nazis, or the Italian Fascists, are used as examples to try and make us wary of patriotism and patriots. Of course, the Nazis, Italian Fascists and their ilk merit strong opprobrium. But using them repeatedly to tar patriotism itself is, honestly, unfortunate. What would you call those, who use the examples of Mao and Stalin, the worst mass-murderers of the twentieth century, to tar all Marxists; Or those who cite genocidal maniacs like Timur, Alauddin Khilji and Aurangzeb, to argue that all of Islam is fanatical? Patently biased, right? Why is it different from patriotism?

You may argue, why bother with liberal harangues on patriotism when liberalism seems to be losing the argument globally, and nationalists seem to be winning? Because in this age of global information flows, high immigration and multi-cultural exchange, liberalism is needed more than ever. And, if I might also state, the idea of a democratic nation-state is the best defender of liberalism in the present day. Liberals must realize that it is in their selfish interest to defend patriotism as well as the nation-state.

Why is the democratic nation-state important for liberalism?

Without the order enforced by a strong institution, the rights of individuals become extremely difficult to uphold. Take child rights: a child's right to life, security, education, food and health. If the institution of the family itself collapses, no amount of 'societal or activist' intervention will adequately compensate. Child rights become theoretical in the absence of a family that protects and supports children. Recall the Rotherham sexual abuses. Over a twenty-year period, this British town experienced the systematic rape, coercive drug abuse, forced prostitution, and involuntary abortions of approximately 1,400 young, mostly white girls, by gangs of mostly Pakistani-British men. It's horrific. Such a large number of young, vulnerable girls. Over such a long period. It is believed that many in the local police and NGO activist circles knew, but remained silent. Apparently, they feared being accused of racism or Islamophobia, keeping in mind the identity of the criminals. But the real shocker lies elsewhere. For what were the families of these poor girls doing? Why didn't they protect their children? The first line of defence for young, vulnerable children is their parents. But unfortunately, often in the blind pursuit of individualism, family structures have seen an erosion in modern times. And resultantly, children don't have the emotional sanctuary of home and family.

Rights cannot survive in a vacuum. They need strong institutions to protect them. And just like children need committed parents, individual citizens need a strong nation-state to protect their rights.

It can be argued that not all parents are caring and protective. But most parents are. And therefore, we would agree that a strong family is good for a child. Similarly, there are authoritarian nation-states which oppress their citizens. But data indicates clearly that a democratic nation-state protects the individual rights of citizens, far more than an authoritarian state does. It is an institution with the power, tools and motivation (driven by citizen votes and democratic protests), to guarantee individual rights, which is the basis for liberalism. A modern democratic nation-state is the best example of political organization that is available today for protecting individual human rights, as compared to any other form of government in history. As Winston Churchill pithily remarked: '… democracy is the worst form of government except for all those other forms that have been tried from time to time.'

If a democratic nation-state, imperfect as it is, is the best guarantor for liberalism and individual rights, then how does one build it? A nation-state, especially a democratic one, is built on a social contract; on the collective belief of a sufficiently large number of people that they are a nation.

So, what makes this collective belief possible? In one simple word: patriotism.

By providing the emotional energy for a nation-state, patriotism also becomes a guarantor for the protection of individual rights and liberalism.

Patriotism can be built on various models. The European model is built on ethnicity, language and religion (different versions of Christianity). The Middle-Eastern model is built on a mix of authoritarianism (of a monarchy or the army) and religion (Sunni or Shia Islam; though, admittedly, some states like Egypt were secular till some time back). Nation-states, in the basic design of their nationhood, are fundamentally exclusionary. They define themselves by what they are NOT. And this aspect, in the minds of most liberals, makes the nation-state an enemy of liberalism. Many European states have, no doubt, become far more inclusive over the recent decades. But this shaking up of the basis of their nationhood, in terms of ethnicity, language and religion, has also shaken their concept of nationhood itself. Many modern global liberal elite speak of a post-nationalism world. John Lennon 'imagined' us living as one, someday. Beautiful. But, as yet, a dream that seems unrealizable in the foreseeable future. That someday is heartbreakingly far away. At this point in time, it seems that liberalism and individual rights cannot exist without the guarantee of a nation-state.

This is where the Indian model appears very interesting. India is one of the few countries in the world, besides probably China and Japan, that can lay claim to being a civilizational-state. This is a fundamentally different model: a collective belief in an ancient civilizational way in which we can imagine India. Some deracinated Indians may believe that India was created by the British, before which we didn't exist as a nation. This is an incomplete understanding of nation-building. Our nationhood is not of the European or Middle-Eastern exclusionary style; and this gives strength to our model in this modern, multicultural world. Our nation is not defined by one language. It is not defined by one religion. It is not defined by one ethnicity. It is defined by a civilization, in which multiple languages, religions and ethnicities have lived together for centuries, and a few for millennia, developing bonds and a deep attachment to this great land. We are not defined by who we are NOT. We are defined by who we are: inheritors of a great civilization that is like our Mother.

This is what makes us, to use Nassim Nicholas Taleb's term, an 'anti-fragile' nation. We can very easily adapt to the rapid pace of change that is a given in these times, and yet keep our core together. Our patriotism is not exclusionary. And our belief in our nation is ancient. The millennia-old *Vishnu Purana* has recorded so beautifully: '*Uttaram Yat Samudrasya Himadreschaiva Dakshinam. Varsham Tad Bharatam Nama Bharati Yatra Santatih*'. North of the ocean, and south of the Himalayas, lies the noble nation of Bharat, and there live the descendants of Bharat.

Not only is the belief in our nationhood ancient, but it is also deeply liberal and inclusive. India accepted refugees from across the world. In ancient times she gave refuge to the Parsees escaping Arab attacks, and Jews fleeing Roman oppression. Even today, Hindu pilgrims visit Ajmer Sharif and Muslims worship at Venkateswara temple.

We are tough. Unlike many other ancient cultures that have died out over the last 1,500 years, we fought back brutal invaders and stubbornly survived. We were also immensely successful. As British economist Angus Maddison noted, India's GDP was the highest in the world for fifteen of the last twenty centuries. India has more non-printing press manuscripts—three million—than the rest of the ancient world combined; this is a marker of the massive knowledge production of the ancient Indians.

Armed with pride, powered with a rebellious innovative spirit, and infused with the spirit of patriotism, India can take its rightful place once again in the comity of nations. And if our motherland prospers, so shall we. If we infuse ourselves with positive patriotism, we will revive a society that is liberal, powerful and inclusive.

A patriotic spirit towards our ancient motherland is not only the sentimental thing to do, but it is also the smart thing to do. It is not just my heart that swells with pride, but even my mind that gets focused, when I say these beautiful words: *Bharat Mata ki Jai!* Glory to Mother India!

First published in *India Today* in August 2019, on the occasion of India's Independence Day celebrations

Dissecting Modernization

Many Indian millennials in the country today are looking outside our culture to find solutions for modern-day issues that they grapple with daily. Some look particularly to the West. But what if I were to tell you that you do not have to look too far to learn about harmonious modern ways of living? What if I were to tell you that your highly liberal role models, who thought way ahead of their times, reside much closer to home? Yes, the modern role models and the highly 'futuristic' ways of living are buried in our own past. Ancient Indian mythology and theology promote concepts that are in tune with many needs of modern society. Let's dive into some examples and look at how we can take a cue and learn from our own traditions to lay the building blocks of a futuristic social set-up.

Freedom of Expression

There is no translation for the English word 'blasphemy' in Vedic Sanskrit, the language of ancient India. This signifies that speaking your mind about Gods, sacred things and religious practices wasn't curbed. The same is depicted by an incident in the *Natya Shastra*, the over 2,000-year-old text describing performing arts in ancient India. In this text, an account is given of the first play that was ever performed, which was, apparently, insulting to some of the divine beings in the audience. They were agitated and wanted the performance stopped. But they were prevented from doing so by Lord Brahma. He conveyed to them that what takes place within the boundaries of the stage is sacred and the performers have the liberty to say what they want. Freedom of expression at its finest.

Women's Rights

One of our ancient scriptures clearly states that the Gods abandon the land where women aren't respected. The *Rig Veda* highlights the presence of rishikas—women rishis—in Vedic times. To give a little context, during the Vedic period, rishis were revered and held the highest status in society. They were, in some ways, akin to the prophets and messiahs of the Abrahamic faiths. This directly indicates what an evolved society it must have been where women were respected and held the highest position of reverence. Furthermore, the names of some of the rishikas, as mentioned in our ancient scriptures, when loosely translated mean 'independent', 'auspicious', 'limitless', 'courageous' and 'scholarly'; signifying that they thrived in an equal social set-up. This culture needs to be revived in modern India. 'Equal' is the key term here; not pro-man or pro-woman but equal. For equality forms the very crux of positive feminism; only in a society where both men and women are treated as equals will everyone peacefully move towards prosperity.

Caste System

In ancient India, hierarchies were not based on birth, but on karma; which ensured that individuals progressed based on merit. For example, Maharishi Valmiki wasn't born a Brahmin but he still went on to attain one of the most revered positions in society, that of a rishi. Similarly, Maharishi Satyakam Jabali was the son of a single Shudra woman. But his intellectual brilliance ensured that he attained one of the highest honours in Lord Ram's kingdom and becoming a rishi.

Technological developments in the field of genetic research today have made it possible to prove that there was no birth-based caste system in ancient India. Modern genetic research has shown that intermingling (i.e., children born from inter-marriage) between different genetic groups was quite common in ancient India. And this intermingling between different genetic groups stopped somewhere around 1,500–2,000 years ago. Intriguingly, this also corresponds to the period that Dr Ambedkar had postulated the caste system became rigid and birth-based. So, it seems quite clear that ancient India was not casteist. The system we have today, where hierarchy is decided by birth, is one that is a corruption of our ancient way.

LGBT Rights

Various Hindu texts and scriptures refer to LGBTs and also showcase the relative acceptance of sexual differences in people to the extent that it was a non-issue. For example, King Bhangaswan changed his gender and turned into a woman, without his choice being curtailed, and went on to give birth to many children.

Similarly, the founder of the Chandravanshi clan, Ilaa, born a girl, changed into a man later—called Ila. In fact, one of the names of ancient India was Illaavarta, in honour of Ilaa.

Even the Smritis—various law books penned down at different stages in time—have been fairly liberal towards homosexuality.

All the above instances show that many answers to the future lie in our past, in our ancient scriptures. Indian myths and ancient texts actually aid the cause of liberalism. By being liberal and open-minded, we are not being less Indian; we are in fact being more Indian. We are, in fact, honouring our great ancestors.

First published in Buzzfeed News, May 2017

Teaching the Bhagavad Gita in Indian Schools

Semitic religions—Judaism, Christianity and Islam—created a Great Separation a few millennia ago with the advent of the Jealous God; this God was jealous of all other Gods, despite having made jealousy one of the seven deadly sins. In Prophet Isaiah's vision, the ecstatic cry of the believers is: '*Yahwey is Other! Other! Other!*' Karen Armstrong calls this 'otherness' a radical separation.

These new religions were centred on faith and one God. Pre-dating them were spiritual paths centred on the impulse to seek; to decode life and living. These approaches combined philosophical wisdom with symbolic, intuitive tools like stories, idols and rituals. They straddled the world, confidently exploring and intermingling. The Gods and Goddesses of Olympus and mystical schools of Egypt attracted minds from all corners, as did the gurukuls and sages on the banks of the Indus and Ganga, leaving liberal space for many paths (such as nature, worship, Goddesses, worship, atheism, etc.).

The Indian path was a menu-based matrix of seeking (gyaan), action (karma), and devotion (bhakti).

Sadly, modern Indian education sought to indoctrinate rather than create seekers; indoctrinate with a colonial interpretation of India's antiquity and culture. Macaulay in his *Minute on Education* visualized 'Brown sahebs' and the English Education Act was passed in 1835 under Lord Bentinck. It systematically removed 'useless' Sanskrit and Persian learning in our pathshalas, gurukuls and madrassas, replacing it with 'useful learning'. Dharam Pal in *The Beautiful Tree* (his work is based on eighteenth-century British records of our education system) writes that our ancient system was destroyed by the British. We began to learn Euclid and Pythagoras, discarding Baudhayana, Pingala, Aryabhatta and Bhaskaracharya. We learnt the four seasons of Europe, discarding learning our six seasons: vasant, grishma, varshaa, sharad, hemant, sheet…

This rejection of our roots continued post-Independence. We were extensively taught the history of our Turk/Mongol/British invaders while Shivaji, Rajendra Chola, Krishnadeva Raya, Ranjit Singh, and Lalitaditya among others were reduced to cursory paragraphs. The English-speaking elite was schooled in Shakespeare, Wordsworth and Homer, ignoring Kalidasa, Thiruvalluvar, Mirza Ghalib and most grievously, sages Vyasa and Valmiki.

In light of this, should the Gita be taught in schools?

Oxford and Cambridge, for most of their existence, primarily imparted religious instruction. As did several US universities, when founded. Only in the relatively recent past have subjects beyond theology been introduced; in addition, not displacement. Greece teaches the writings of Homer and Hesiod. New Zealand and Australia teach aboriginal stories and symbology with proud acceptance. Egypt introduces their citizens to ancient Egyptian mystical symbology and concepts.

Why not India?

The Gita is a subset of Mahabharat. And Mahabharat and Ramayan are the two foundational epics of our land; the land of dharma and Indic religions of Hinduism, Buddhism, Jainism, Sikhism, and Indian Islam and Indian Christianity. They are intuitively more liberal at their core than the Western and Middle-Eastern approaches to religion. The recent Pew religious survey has unsurprisingly indicated that a distinct majority of Indian Muslims and Christians believe in dharma and karma—two central tenets of the Gita.

It would surprise many to know that Ramayan and Mahabharat were taught not only in gurukuls and pathshalas but also in madrassas, till as late as the eighteenth century (with few exceptions in between).

An interesting aside: the original copies of the Indian Constitution in 1950 were illustrated with Nandlal Bose's art, depicting scenes from the two beloved Indian epics. Yes, Ramayan and Mahabharat. Why? Our Constituent Assembly of fifteen women and 284 men were crystal clear that 'India that is Bharat' was not born in 1947, but is a continuing civilizational Republic. These stories are our roots. And a connection to the roots is critical for growth. *And*, this connection must be with *our* roots. Not foreign roots. Unfortunately, the Bhagavad Gita was not included in our school curricula in 1950.

Many schools already teach moral science, drawn from the Bible and Western concepts of morality. Let us expand this canvas and also teach Amir Khusrau Dahlawi, who wrote:

> *The face glows with the light of faith alongside flowing locks of dark hair.*
> *Every belief is candescent; I can be a Hindu one day, a Muslim the next.*

Let us teach Mir Taqi Meer, who wrote:

> *From that divine beauty sparkles light for all,*
> *Whether it is the evening of the Kaaba or the lamp of the Somnath temple.*

And, let us teach the Gita.

Indians already know parts of the Gita without being formally taught in schools. They quote the Gita. They use examples from the Gita. It is our ancient, continuing living tradition. Lord Krishna and Arjun have found space on our movie screens and theatre grounds. Lord Krishna and Radha permeate our festivals and intercalate the spaces within our cultural lattice.

In our elitist misguided disdain for our ancient culture, we have discarded our wisdom-infused heritage. This has led to some deracinated and disconnected English-speaking Indians. It is time to undo this damage. Let us teach the Gita, Ramayan and Mahabharat to our school children. It is inclusive. It is wise. It offers guidance. Most importantly, *hamaara hai! It is ours.*

First published in *The Times of India*, April 2022

History

The Myth of the Aryan Invasion Theory

A South Indian politician recently accused a North Indian colleague of being an Aryan invader. At first I was tempted to dismiss it as yet another case of politicking. Politicians, after all, will do what politicians do. Some condemn Turkic/Mongol invaders, others British invaders and then there are those who move on to Aryan invaders. It's a free country; one can nurse grudges against assorted invaders of the past. Having said that, it has nothing to do with Indians living in the twenty-first century. That's obvious.

My surprise, though, lay in this politician believing, without any trace of doubt, in the Aryan invasion theory (AIT). What is AIT? History books tell us that the Indus or Harappan civilization was peopled by dark-skinned Dravidians (the name was a later addition; initially they were called 'indigenous people') who were invaded by fair-skinned Aryans from Central Asia/Eastern Europe around 3,500 years ago. The Aryans, we are told, massacred and then pushed the remaining Dravidians to the south, occupied the freed land, and composed the Vedas along with a vast body of other Sanskrit texts. They also invented the caste system to oppress the Dravidians. This AIT theory appealed to the British colonialists, who were struck by the 'romantic' parallel of a fresh wave of new white-skinned invaders, repeating an ancient story.

AIT is largely based on linguistics, i.e., the study of languages. European scholars of the colonial era found striking similarities between Sanskrit and Iranian/European languages, suggesting a common source or intermingling. Many theories were propounded to explain this intriguing discovery, one of them being the Aryan invasion theory. Another was the out-of-India theory, suggesting that people moved out from their homeland, India, in a north-west direction, and carried their language with them. There were other theories as well. Unfortunately, languages don't have return addresses, so one can find enough arguments to support all theories. Linguistics is regarded as a science by some (many others may disagree), but it has inherent limitations compared to other, more rigorous scientific disciplines. Theories based on linguistics are open to interpretations. Unfortunately, the debate in this area is also conducted in our usual 'mature' fashion (*sarcasm alert*). Linguistic-driven historians, instead of debating publicly and with a scholarly attitude, indulge in name-calling. Insults are bandied about with abandon and callousness. It is unfortunate.

Linguistics, due to its very nature, may open the field to contradictory 'conjectures', but fortunately there are other scientific disciplines available today, to help us evaluate the AIT issue.

Archaeology examines history through site excavations and analysis of artefacts/physical remains. Invaders tend to leave a trail of destruction; so if there was an invasion, there has to be archaeological evidence of it. Unfortunately, for the proponents of AIT, there is little credible archaeological evidence of a violent invasion 3,500 years ago. Seeing the sands shift beneath their irresolute feet, some proponents of AIT pirouetted and propounded a new Aryan migration theory (AMT), i.e., the so-called Aryans peacefully sauntered into India and most of the so-called Dravidians of the heavily-populated Indus civilization moved south voluntarily. If this were true, there would have been a massive influx of Eastern Europeans/Central Asians into India at the time, right? Which would show up in genetic records?

Unfortunately for the (now) AMT proponents, genetic science disproves this hypothesis. Most major papers on Indian genetics published in scientific journals like *Nature* and *American Journal of Human Genetics* over the last few years agree on one thing: there was no significant addition to the Indian gene pool 3,500 years ago!

So, let us summarize: AIT/AMT proponents ask us to believe that there was this small bunch of nomadic people called the Aryans who came to India 3,500 years ago. It was too minuscule a band to show up in any archaeological or genetic records. And this tiny group did not indulge in any mass violence. But somehow, these mythical supermen managed to, peacefully, convince the far more populous, advanced and urbane Dravidians to migrate en masse to south India. Presumably they debated the so-called Dravidians into abandoning their homes. And while doing so, these nomadic 'Aryan barbarians' also overturned the entire linguistic and cultural landscape of India. Moreover, this allegedly foreign culture was so comprehensively absorbed, that it survives to this day, thousands of years later, across the country. Honestly, does this make any sense? Consider another paradox we are asked to swallow unquestioningly: the so-called Dravidians who built the greatest civilization of its time (called the Harappan/Indus civilization today), left no literature at all. On the other hand, these nomadic-barbarian 'Aryans', with no settled homeland, created the largest body of literature, philosophical and technical texts of that era. Creating narratives of *history* to reconcile these huge contradictions leads to more contortions than in a *jalebi*.

Paraphrasing the principle of Occam's razor, the simpler explanation is probably true: there was probably no race called the Aryans. The Harappan/Indus and the Vedic cultures were likely one and the same. And most of us in India today, north and south, are, in high probability, descendants of that culture.

Indian children need to be taught that there are serious and credible doubts among many historians (not just Indian, but global) about the Aryan invasion theory. These alternative theories, based on archaeology and genetics, which largely do not support AIT, must also be taught. Then let students, as well as future generations, make up their own minds.

I, for one, tend to agree with what a European friend once remarked. That the Aryan invasion theory is the greatest piece of fiction concocted by Europeans since the ethereal plays of Shakespeare. Perhaps it's time to close the book!

First published in *The Times of India,* December 2015

Young, Indian and Insolent

I ran into a politician the other day who's not your average *neta*. He's not young, but has a modern, reformist outlook. This is why I was surprised with what followed. He said to me that one of the problems in India is that the youth are too insolent and rebellious. They are not willing to listen, even to 'sensible' ideas. Furthermore, he opined, since we are a democracy and the vast majority of our voters are youngsters 'who don't listen', it's difficult to get things done. This was followed with what I consider a tired old cliché from the past: 'Today's youth don't know Indian culture. They don't even respect their elders.' That set me thinking. Was this politician right? Are the Indian youth somehow less Indian when compared to their parents?

I didn't get a chance to interact with too many youngsters when I worked in the insurance industry. They aren't really interested in insurance; to be honest, even adults aren't interested in insurance! As an author I have had occasion to interact with many young people, since a vast majority of my readers fall in that group. So, do I agree with the politician, that today's youth are insolent and rebellious? Yes, they are. They respect you only if they think you deserve it. If they don't respect you, they make it obvious, regardless of your age or position. But I do not think this is a problem. In fact, I believe the insolence of our youth is our competitive advantage. Furthermore, I think they are reviving a significant aspect of ancient Indian culture by being insolent and rebellious. They are, if anything, more Indian than their parents.

Let's turn to our ancient past to understand what Indian culture stood for.

A famous incident from the Mahabharat (it has also been described in the *Vayu Purana*, among others), is held up as an example of the misfortune that befalls those who don't listen to their elders. The great king Yayati was cursed with old age for a sin he had committed. He asked his five sons if one among them would offer to exchange his youth with his father's old age. The eldest son, Yadu, refused, saying to his father, 'It's your sin, not mine.' The youngest son, Puru, readily agreed to be the 'good son' and let Yayati become young while he himself aged rapidly. So how did King Yayati react? He punished the son who stood up to him and blessed the one who indulged him. Yadu was cursed that his descendants would be destroyed and they would never be kings. The lazy observer would believe that this is why the descendants of Yadu, the Yadavs, went on to destroy themselves in a fratricidal civil war. The descendants of Puru, amongst whom are the Pandavs and the Kauravs, went on to constitute the great dynasty that ruled large parts of ancient India. Therefore, the moral of this story was seemingly clear: be like Puru; listen to your elders. The rebellious, like Yadu, suffer—in fact, even your future progeny may suffer for your sin of rebellion. Pretty comprehensive punishment!

I am not questioning the story but its contemporary interpretation. Let's delve deeper into its message. Did Yadu's descendants really suffer ignominy? Quite the contrary. One of his descendants, Kartavirya Arjun (different from the Arjun in the Mahabharat) ruled the entire Vedic world. The civil war that destroyed the Yadav royalty occurred *after* the descendants of the 'good son' Puru, the Pandavs and Kauravs, had already destroyed themselves in a civil war that is known today through one of our great epics, the Mahabharat. So if you pay attention to the nuances in the story, the descendants of both Yadu and Puru experienced triumphs as well as terrible calamities. In fact, one can even argue that Yadu was actually blessed, since one of his descendants was the great God, Lord Krishna Himself!

People enjoy good fortune or suffer misfortune based on their own karma, not on whether they submit themselves to the powerful. This lesson is revealed in various scriptures of all religions. You should bow your head only to the Gods and Goddesses. Everyone else has to earn your respect, and you in turn have to earn theirs. This is exactly what the modern Indian youth believe.

So what is the lesson for the traditional elite in modern India? Many of these groups—upper castes of all religions (the caste system in India exists within Hinduism, Christianity and Islam), men, politicians, bureaucrats, senior media and legal figures, elders, hereditary rich—have got used to the excessive and easy deference that they have been treated with for far too long. They need to adapt to a new scenario where they are now being challenged. They will have to work hard to retain the status they've gotten used to.

As for the youth, I say go ahead and rebel if you see wrong. If your elders disrespect women, rebuke them. If your politicians are corrupt, protest and vote them out. If your religious leaders preach hatred, tell them they are wrong and argue against their extremist interpretation of the scriptures. But rebellion is a lot more than opposition for its own sake. It's also about your life.

When you study the subjects that you want to, rather than what you are told to, it is healthy rebellion. When you start your own company and succeed, regardless of the naysayers, that too is rebellion. When you work hard and make your own living, rather than live off the money inherited from your parents, it is rebellion laced with self-respect. When you marry the person you love, regardless of religious or community divides, it is the most beautiful rebellion. The root of all creativity is rebellion.

But remember that if rebellion uses violence and verbal abuse, it's hooliganism, *goondagardi*. The moment you resort to violence, you lose the moral high-ground and transform into those you are rebelling against. Also, rebellion without a sense of personal duty and purpose often leads to chaos, as is evident in India's recent past. Besides expecting others to earn your respect, you must be alive to the responsibility of deserving respect, through your conduct. So go ahead and rebel, but always within the constraints of the law and always with a sense of purpose.

I'd love to see an even more rebellious and insolent India. For that would be a precursor to a great India!

First published in *Hindustan Times*, 2013

British Bombay, *Aamchi* Mumbai

A standard criticism that every Indian city faces, especially Mumbai, is that it is very dirty. The air is polluted, the sewage and drainage system creaks, greenery is minimal and there is muck and garbage everywhere. Despite being a proud Mumbaikar, I'm constrained to admit that these criticisms are valid. Mercifully, we've lately begun to discuss these issues seriously; green shoots of improvement have sprouted hesitatingly. As the nation grows increasingly wealthy, things are bound to get better. I believe that.

The strange thing about this criticism, though, are murmurs suggesting that the British colonial administrators of our city were better. That Bombay (as Mumbai was known in the British/early independence era), was cleaner and better organized with grand buildings and leafy roads.

It set me thinking: does cleanliness only apply to external surroundings, or is it also related to the intangibles, for instance, karma? Yes, the Asiatic–Gothic buildings of the British era in south Mumbai are beautiful. It might interest you to know, though, that karmically they are far dirtier than any modern Mumbai building. Let me elaborate.

Consider the karma of the current 'Indian' Mumbai. We contribute over 6 per cent to India's GDP and 30 per cent to its income tax collections. Mumbai has a work ethic that is the envy of India and requires little ratification. We have faced disasters, ranging from terrorist attacks to floods, but the resilient Mumbai spirit gets us back on our feet in no time. We have lapsed into the temporary insanity of communal violence at times, but have returned to our senses admirably fast. Despite an undermanned police force and a paralysed court system, Mumbai's violent crime rate is a tiny fraction of what occurs in New York or Boston. The entire state of Maharashtra, and indeed, much of India, depends on the wealth and resources that Mumbai generates. A friend once remarked that Maharashtra and India stand on Mumbai's broad shoulders. Hyperbolic though the statement may be, it is not far from the truth. The karma of Indian Mumbai is clean, it is good.

Let's now turn to the received story of British Bombay. The then king of Great Britain, Charles II obtained the seven islands that later comprised Bombay city, as dowry from Catherine of Portugal in 1662. These islands were inhabited by Indians for millennia, but were not significantly relevant until then. We are also told that the British were master tradesmen who transformed British Bombay into a land of gold. A casual mention is made of some 'intolerance' towards locals, such as not allowing Indians and dogs into hotels. Overall though, we are told, British Bombay emerged as among the wealthiest cities in the world due to the white man's efficiency and entrepreneurial brilliance.

Be that as it may, this is a tale that has been carefully airbrushed by British historians, and sadly, even Indian historians. What was the *actual source* of the massive wealth on which the British built the foundation of this modern city? It was opium smuggling, the largest drug-peddling racket in the history of humanity. The Western world calls it the opium 'trade', as if it were just another commodity covered by the rules of free-trade. Far from it, it was perhaps one of the biggest crimes against humanity ever recorded.

The drug-smuggling business was a key source of initial earnings for the East India Company and indeed the British empire. The British forced Indian farmers to replace food crops with opium, which was then smuggled into China. Artificially engineered food shortages due to forced abandonment of food crops resulted in the death of tens of millions of Indians. Yes, *tens of millions of Indians.* This happened primarily in the eastern parts of the country, in British-manufactured 'famines'. When Indians rebelled, they were brutally put down by the 'Company'. Millions of Chinese also died or were wasted by drug addiction. When the Chinese rebelled, Great Britain declared war on China, defeated them—in what came to be known as the 'Opium Wars'—and coerced them into accepting the drug-smuggling business. Hong Kong and Canton were the primary bases for this disgusting business in China, while British Calcutta and British Bombay were the primary centres in India. Sadly, some Chinese and Indian businessmen collaborated in this rape of their motherlands. Some of those business houses survive to this day; many of them in India cleansed their drug-smuggling history with philanthropic karma. But the British, the originators, drivers and captains of this crime against humanity, did no karmic atonement. Practically all educated Chinese know this sad story, but most educated Indians do not. British Bombay was at the heart of a business that directly led to the devastation of two ancient civilizations.

Today's Mumbai, *aamchi* Mumbai, may be physically dirtier and have less greenery, but we are getting our mojo back, slowly but surely. Grand buildings are coming up once again. The city's infrastructure is improving, again, slowly but surely. People from all over India come to this city of dreams to build their life and earn money. But most importantly, in 'Indian' Mumbai, we earn money cleanly, and not the way the British did; we do not earn money from practices that would even horrify the universe. Our karma is clean. We, the people of *aamchi* Mumbai, have to a large extent, cleaned up the karmic muck that the British had accumulated in these seven great islands.

And yes, that physical cleanliness thing, we'll do that too. Give us time.

First published in *India Today*, April 2015

Divide and Rule Laws in Modern India

The Preamble to our Constitution succinctly lays down its guiding purpose, one being: EQUALITY of status and of opportunity. No society is (or has ever been) truly equal, it being an ever-elusive aspiration for one and all. It helps though, if the first step is 'equality before the law'. All civilized countries practice equality before the law; this ideally should entail the law not differentiating based on religious beliefs. We proudly profess to be a secular state; it would follow, therefore, that our laws must treat all Indians as equal, regardless of religious beliefs. Regrettably, this is not so.

At this point you'd be forgiven for thinking that this article is about the Uniform Civil Code (UCC): one law for all in matters of marriage, divorce, inheritance and adoption. It's not. No doubt Dr B.R. Ambedkar had drafted into the Directive Principles of our Constitution the need for a Uniform Civil Code. Notwithstanding that, we have different personal laws for religious communities. Some tend to portray this as appeasement of Muslims. I fail to understand that. Appeasement would entail being favoured over and above others, or having superior rights as compared to others. In fact, Muslim women have inferior rights when compared to their Hindu and Christian sisters. It is the appeasement of a few antediluvian male Muslim leaders alone. A vast majority of Muslim society actually suffers.

But the problem isn't restricted to personal laws alone. I would like to draw your attention to the sectarian bias that is inbuilt in other laws as well. Many of these laws find their origin in the British colonial era. Sadly, many more have been formulated by the Indian ruling elite since Independence.

For instance, Hindus are granted tax benefits through the Hindu Undivided Family (HUF) principle, which are not available to Muslims and Christians. Many Muslims and Christians complain about this discrimination by the tax authorities. State governments across the country use existing laws to take over Hindu temples from local communities. Not surprisingly, there have often been serious allegations of corruption and maladministration made against many bureaucrats who administer these Hindu temples. Amazingly enough, the government cannot similarly take over Muslim or Christian religious properties, as that is illegal. Many Hindus consequently wonder about their freedom to practice their religion due to this differentiation. The Right to Education (RTE) Act, combined with the sectarian 93rd Amendment, is also a tool for differentiation. For example, the government forces a 25 per cent free-seat quota only on Hindu-run schools (not on non-Hindu schools), which is theoretically supposed to be reimbursed by the government. In practice, often the reimbursement is delayed or denied. Due to this and other such policies, thousands of Hindu-run schools have been forced to shut down. The 93rd Amendment/RTE combine also hurt the educational interests of scheduled castes and tribes grievously by restricting reservation benefits for them in many government-aided minority educational institutions. Ironically, some minorities too are discontented. Owing to differentiation in the RTE, minority-run schools can appoint teachers without the standard Teachers Eligibility Test (TET) in Maharashtra, which has led to allegations of hiring unqualified teachers.

Consider the Maharashtra Anti-Superstition Act. Allegedly a 'rationalist law', in practice this Act often targets and bans 'superstitions' that are more widely prevalent among low-caste Hindus, Ajlaf/Arzal Muslims and low-class Christians. This law rarely targets the superstitions of upper-caste Hindus, Ashraf Muslims or upper-class/white-skinned Christians. For example, an obscure Christian pastor was arrested recently for claiming disease-cures through miracles. However, Mother Teresa was celebrated for doing exactly the same thing; in fact, those professed miracles actually led to her canonization. The Aghoris (treated as outcastes by some) are probably the only religious group in India whose freedom to practice their faith has been legally banned under this same law.

What do you think is the impact of such laws that clearly differentiate between different communities? As you can imagine, it leads to strife and resentment. You may have noted that when *jallikattu* (bull-fighting) was banned by the courts, many Tamil Hindus asked, angrily, why the Muslim Bakr Eid was not banned. Why would the courts consider bull-fighting, in which the animal rarely dies, more cruel than the ritual mass slaughter of animals without any stunning or other pain mitigation? Having said that, the Muslim community did not ask for a ban on *jallikattu*. Why blame them?

Such laws and policies were originally designed by a colonial power such that it would create fissures and friction between communities. Thereafter, the elite *'gora maai-baap'* (British authorities) would move in and 'broker peace' among the warring communities; and use those very divisions to perpetuate their rule. History books called it the divide-and-rule policy. The British were master practitioners of it.

The misfortune of India is that the post-Independence ruling elite (comprising some politicians and academics, some in the national media and legal community, some NGOs and a few bureaucrats) has continued this policy of divide-and-rule. We need to break this cycle.

And the best way to do so is to protest against every single divide-and-rule law that differentiates between Indians, based on their religious beliefs; and have it repealed. There should also be a constitutional amendment that the Parliament cannot enact any law, nor the courts pronounce any judgment, that differentiates between communities based on religious beliefs.

It's been nearly seventy years since the British left this soil. It's about time we rose above the games they played.

First published in *The Times of India,* May 2016

Forgive … Don't Forget History

One of the greatest gifts that children can receive from their parents is an emotionally stable childhood. Materialistic trappings cannot compensate for the bliss of growing up in a well-adjusted, happy family; one in which the child is not exposed to warring parents, domestic violence, physical or emotional abuse. Sadly, both research and anecdotal evidence indicate that many children are deprived of this blessing and grow up in dysfunctional families. Resultantly, they develop coping skills, albeit situational, to handle traumatic experiences: sometimes denial (convincing their conscious mind that no abuse happened) and at other times, unfocussed anger (allowing inner rage to poison their mind to the extent that they become hateful, even towards those unrelated to the abuse). One doesn't need to be a psychologist to know that both approaches are unhealthy.

As it is with children, so it is with countries. Few can rightfully claim that they have no 'history' to contend with. But it is easier to gaze charitably at the past with quiet confidence when the country is successful. During my recent travels across the US on a fellowship programme, it was apparent that the Anglo-Saxon American mind was unscathed by the oppression of British colonial rule (the African-American mind is another matter). My journey through the Arab world however, told a different tale. They still cringe at the memory of the persecution and oppression they suffered for centuries under Mongol, Turkish and European conquests. The present-day outbursts of 'unfocussed anger' in the Arab world could well be strongly associated with this historical abuse—besides other issues, I admit.

The psychological concept of 'denial' however—in which the victim convinces himself that no (or minimal) abuse happened—finds almost matchless expression in India. One example of this is the attitude of many Indians towards the British Raj.

Many believe that while there may have been some injustices meted out during the British Raj, overall, colonial rule was beneficial. Some even claim that the British created India, as, apparently, we weren't 'one people' till they arrived. When one draws up a list of the excesses of the British Raj, the worst, we are told, was the Jallianwala Bagh massacre, in which over 1,000 Indians were killed in cold blood. But is this the worst they did? Not by a long shot. In the early 1940s, Churchill consciously ordered a scorched earth policy in eastern India to halt the advancing Japanese army, which led to the death of, credible estimates suggest, between 1.5 to four million Indians. That's nearly as many as the number of Jews that Hitler ordered to their deaths. *Late Victorian Holocausts* by Mike Davis gives troubling accounts of the vast numbers—in the millions—killed by British policies. A little known fact in India is that the edifice of the British Raj (and the white man's 'civilizing mission') was built on the biggest drug-running racket in the history of humanity (also see British Bombay, *Aamchi* Mumbai, page 147). The British forced Indian farmers to grow opium, which was then smuggled into China. The Chinese economy—not to mention the lives of millions of Chinese—was destroyed through this trade. At the same time, millions of Indians died as food crops were forcibly replaced with opium (besides some other cash crops that suited British trade), leading to recurring food shortages and famines.

These events have been carefully airbrushed from Indian history books. Why? Some enthusiastic voices allege that those who have dominated the Indian imagination for most of its independent history—the Indian anglicized elite—have obscured these facts deliberately out of a sense of loyalty to the country of their 'cultural' forefathers: Great Britain. But that would be too grave and adventurous a charge. I have interacted with many members of the anglicized elite. I admit that it is sometimes difficult to understand their strangely eccentric culture, but they are no traitors. They do love India in their own peculiar way; although many of them believe that Indians cannot handle the truth and 'social peace' can only be maintained by 'airbrushing' history to remove the ugly portions. Besides the British era, this patronizing 'photoshopping' effort has also been directed at other painful historical events, like the brutal Turkic invasions of India in the medieval period, rated as one of history's bloodiest conquests (read *Tarikh-i-Ferishta* to know more).

Denial invariably leads to repressed truth finding expression in the ugliness of hatred and anger, as we see in some parts of India today. It's healthier in the long run for societies to accept, confront and then learn to handle the truth. Forgive, but do not forget. Our history books must factually cover in detail, the famines engineered by British policies; as also the massive British drug-smuggling business. We should truthfully reveal to Indian students the horrific brutality of medieval Turkic invaders. But we must also teach that history should not extend itself into the present and colour our perceptions of a people today. For example, we don't need to settle scores with today's England for the actions of their ancestors. And furthermore, if Indian Christians are not blamed for British excesses just because the British happened to be Christians, why should Indian Muslims be blamed for the vicious Turkic/Mongol/Persian conquests, just because these foreigners happened to be Muslims? We were slaves under foreign rule for centuries. Let's not blame our fellow Indians for the crimes of those barbaric foreigners.

Many civilizations have at some point of time been victims, and at other times, oppressors. Present conduct, rather than past actions, should determine the way a people are judged today, if at all.

My suggestion: examine honestly the troubling episodes of our history; accept the truth and learn from it. Forgive, but do not forget. This truth will kill the poison that is coursing through the veins of a few extremists in India.

Denial is not a cure for historical abuse. Truth is. *Satyameva Jayate*.

First published in *Hindustan Times*, November 2014

States vs Centre

'We are going in the wrong direction!' How often have we heard this in the recent past when talk veers to India's future? There is an overriding and all-pervasive atmosphere of pessimism that surrounds us today. No doubt, there are short-term political issues, and these have been analysed in detail by people far wiser in such matters than I can ever be. I'm sure that as a country, we will find solutions to our political problems.

Let me focus instead on a long-term issue in this article. It has been much lamented that the root cause of our mis-governance is the coalition era we are forced to contend with. Even among rational, thoughtful people, there is a deep concern with the leaching away of power from Delhi to the states. We long for a single-party dominance, because we are convinced that only then will we see results. Do I agree? Frankly, I don't.

How many times in our civilizational history has some powerful ruler stamped his mark over most of the Indian subcontinent? Not often. In the last two-and-a-half thousand years, more than fifty percent of our land has been ruled by a stable, centralized power for not more than eight hundred years: under the Mauryas, Guptas, Mughals, Marathas, British and the first forty years post our independence.

There have been some bewildering interpretations proffered for this historical fact, suggesting that India was never really a country and that the British created it for us. In my opinion, this is a jaundiced view. The concept of a nation-state itself didn't exist before the various treaties of Westphalia in the seventeenth century. In sixteenth-century London, if you said you were loyal to England and not to King Henry, you would be beheaded as a traitor. In early and medieval history, 'nations' existed as cultural, civilizational or tribal entities, and not necessarily as political units. Culturally, India has always been one 'country', or civilization. Politically however, we were, more often than not, divided.

That political division was our competitive strength, for it encouraged innovation, the most powerful tool for wealth generation. India was a hotbed of innovation through most of history, and gave birth to millennia-impacting innovations like the place value of numbers and the philosophical concept of karma, along with practical, earthy solutions in areas such as architecture, surgery, ship-building, irrigation techniques and many others. By its very nature, innovation is disruptive and rebellious. Our political divisions allowed our innovators and free-thinkers to explore options. If the Palas didn't like your ideas, you could go to the Cholas. If the Tuluvas of Vijaynagar didn't like your thoughts, you trotted off to the Bahmani Sultans. Since we were culturally one country, travel was easy. Decentralization helped innovation which in turn, kept us rich.

So can we argue the opposite? Does centralization harm innovation? More often than not, yes, it does. A Chinese emperor, who ruled China with an iron hand, banned maritime activities a few decades after Admiral Zheng He's trailblazing fifteenth-century sea voyages. No Chinese dared to rebel against this anti-innovation decision of the emperor. The long-term impact was that it wasn't Chinese ships that powered the colonization of the world, but European ones. Such examples abound in India as well, drawn from periods of over-centralization, for instance, the rejection of the Gutenberg press by Emperor Akbar (otherwise a very good ruler) or our suicidal economic policies from the 1950s to 1991. Had India been politically divided or decentralized at the time, these unfortunate decisions could have been challenged.

So a decentralized, messy and politically divided land is actually good for innovation. The problem with political division, however, is the risk of violence and chaos. This has happened on occasion in India's history. But now, our democracy has given us the tools to manage these political divisions without the concomitant violence. So I say, let power shift to our states; let the Centre become weak. The stunning progress in some states will set up a demonstration effect which can trigger a very healthy competition between different chief ministers. Ruchir Sharma, the author of *Breakout Nations*, has said *(paraphrasing)* that if you want to be pessimistic about India, go to the national capital. If you want to feel optimistic, go to the states.

The forced decentralization that we observe in India today, in part due to weak coalition governments, is good for us. We need to strengthen this trend constitutionally—too many constitutional powers still remain with the Centre. It cannot get things done, but it can obstruct the states from moving ahead. Many items from the union and concurrent lists in the constitution need to be transferred to the states' list. If the states become constitutionally strong, regional parties will not waste their time battling for sops from the Centre—instead, they will spend that time governing their states. And our country will become a hotbed of innovation once again.

The ability to innovate is a far more potent and long-term competitive advantage when compared to raw efficiency. Ask America. Interestingly, the US Constitution has focussed on states' rights, keeping the federal government relatively weak. Equally interestingly, India's modern, and golden-economic period (post 1991) coincides with a political era when no single party won a parliamentary majority on its own. Coincidence? I don't think so.

Does the election of 2014, that threw up a single-party majority government for the first time in twenty-five years, change my mind that a decentralized India is the best way forward? No. And I am delighted to see that there are systemic moves to strengthen the natural decentralization process of the last twenty-five years. The recommendations of the 14th Finance Commission have been accepted. Not only are the states receiving more money, but more importantly, they exercise control over that money. They can determine their priorities and spend accordingly, rather than implement a central scheme designed in Delhi. This process needs to be taken forward; city administrations and gram panchayats must also receive similar powers. Many other powers (and obviously, responsibilities) need to be decentralized as well.

First published in *The Asian Age/Deccan Chronicle*, 2013

May Shakti Be with You!

Groans and sighs! This, in essence, is the usual reaction of the older generation when a conversation veers towards the Indian youth and their apparent disinterest in our culture, religion and country. In the eyes of the elders, India's standards are collapsing because the youth are rushing headlong into a love affair with the West. They're convinced that our culture will get blown away like leaves in the wind by this storm called modernization, and its uncontrollable off-shoots, like the 'very crass' reality TV and unbridled internet. Is this true? Hell no!

The truth is that many from the older generation are in fact the ones who are not in touch with India's ancient culture, which was, at its core, confident and open-minded. Let me give you a few examples (the examples will necessarily have to be very old, because I think India forgot the true essence of its ancient culture in the last few centuries).

Sanskrit is believed to be an unchangeable language. Not true. What we know as Sanskrit today is Classical Sanskrit. In its ancient form, Vedic Sanskrit was a vibrant language with a strong, mathematical structure within which it allowed for flexibility.

Ancient India welcomed refugees and immigrants from across the world. Christianity arrived in India before it went to most countries of Europe. Jews found succour in India more than two millennia ago. Zoroastrians were absorbed by ancient Gujarat. Siddi Muslims, brought in as slaves of the Arabs and Portuguese, escaped their shackles and founded minor kingdoms in western India. India was the America of the ancient world, accepting into its folds the bold, the wretched, the adventurous and the tortured; people who had the spirit and drive to seek better lives.

Foreigners (like the Southeast Asians) adopted Indian names, lifestyle and culture because they were attracted to its vibrancy, just like people from across the world Americanize themselves today. Furthermore, ancient Indians were open to other cultures. The Greeks may have been beaten back when they tried to conquer our land more than 2,000 years ago, but Indians learned the resplendent Gandhara art from the Hellenistic failed-invaders. The famed idlis, unarguably among the most popular of Indian snacks, probably arrived in India from the shores of Indonesia.

Our open-mindedness even extended into the sensitive realm of religion. There are hundreds of versions of India's seminal epic, the Ramayan. Many of these versions differ substantially from one another. Some depict Raavan as a purely evil demon while in others he is an accomplished great ruler and a devoted Shiva bhakt, albeit with faults. Lady Sita is docile and submissive in some depictions, while in others she's conceptualized as fiery and warrior-like. All these different versions of the Ramayan coexisted harmoniously and were equally loved and revered.

Great Sufi Islamic saints found deep similarities between Hinduism and Islam. In his book, *The Mingling of the Two Oceans*, Dara Shikoh, a Mughal prince, drew fascinating parallels between the Muslim Abu Arwah (Father of all souls) and the Hindu *Parmatma* (Supreme soul). The title adopted by one of our greatest emperors, *Jahanpanah* Akbar, was not the usual 'conqueror of the world', but '*refuge of the world*'. The great Mauryas, the most powerful royal family of their time, had many religions coexisting within their family; Chandragupta Maurya was probably a Jain, Bindusara was an Ajivika and Ashok was a Buddhist. Rajaraj Chola was an ardent Shaivite Hindu who patronized the construction of Buddhist viharas.

Numerous such instances reveal to us that we were once an open-minded, curious and accommodating society; and this, precisely, was the secret of our success. A success that was mind-numbing: according to the widely-cited estimates of British economist, Angus Maddison, throughout most of recorded history, India was the richest economy in the world, contributing between 25 per cent and 33 per cent of the world's GDP! The Roman emperor Vespasian had prohibited trade with India because his empire was facing currency shortages as a result of importing Indian goods and paying for them in gold/silver bullion. Despite not possessing massive gold mines, India is known to have amongst the largest quantities of gold hoarded in private hands. Some historians believe that this is the legacy of centuries of gold-bullion-driven trade surpluses which India enjoyed.

What happened to us? How did we fall so dramatically from the dizzying heights that we had occupied for millennia? A popular notion is that foreign conquerors like the Turks and the British did this to us. Not true. They didn't destroy us. We destroyed ourselves.

We lost our mojo because we forgot who we were. We forgot our core culture. We lost our confident open-mindedness. The concept of '*kala-pani*', which banned foreign travel, crept into the Hindu consciousness; ironically, this happened to a people who had produced the greatest seafarers and traders of the ancient era. The self-assured intermingling of religions and cultures that had prevailed for centuries gave way to insecure, exclusivist thoughts. Scientific temper declined, even though science was never in conflict with religion in India. Unlike Japan, we did not capitalize on the great industrial advancements of the Western world. Slowly but surely, what followed was our steady decline. Despite that, India was the second largest economy in the world at the beginning of the British reign. But on a per-capita basis, we were already behind a rapidly rising Europe.

The British only made it obvious that we were in terminal decline, a fact hidden by the immense legacy of our past successes. Merely 1,00,000 British lorded over 300 million Indians for nearly 200 years. Let's be clear, this was not just a conquest. This was humiliation that is unparalleled in human history. It happened because there was a class of Indians that controlled India on behalf of the British. General Dyer may have given the orders to fire at defenceless Indians in Jallianwala Bagh, but the people who actually shot them were our fellow countrymen.

Two closed-minded groups have risen over the landscape of India in the recent past: the India-rejecters and the India-glorifiers. Grant me the indulgence to simplify so I can get the point across. The India-rejecters reject our past. They are nihilistic people who deny their Indian heritage and attempt to impose foreign values and influences, e.g., the Anglophiles, the Marxists. It seems as if they choose to believe that there is nothing (or very little) that is worthwhile about India's ancient past. This argument of the India-rejecters is countered by the India-glorifiers, e.g., the religious extremists. These India-glorifiers are convinced that everything about India's past was perfect, pristine and can never be questioned, much less re-examined. They also seem to think there isn't much that we can learn or adopt from foreign lands.

Both these groups, the India-rejecters and India-glorifiers, are not what India, or even the Indian subcontinent, needs. The Indian elite were primarily composed of the India-rejecters in the first four decades after Independence, and we have seen what economic muddle and intellectual sterility they created in our land. Pakistan, on the other hand, is by now practically in the hands of religious extremists and God help that sorry mess of a country. The ancient Indian culture would have rejected both these extremist groups.

In stark contrast to the previous generation, the youth of today fill my heart with hope. Let me tell you why: because they exhibit the confident open-mindedness that was quintessentially Indian in the past. They are proud of who they are, but are willing to disagree with certain elements of our bequeathed heritage. For example, most of my youth readers have appreciated my not using my caste-surname on the covers of my books, but remain eager to learn more about the brilliance of Lord Shiva. They are proud of their culture, but are willing to explore others' as well, e.g., a Muslim youth conveyed to me that he is a proud Muslim, but he is also inspired by the concept of Har Har Mahadev; a Hindu youngster wrote in to appreciate that I often say Insha'Allah despite being a devout Hindu. Today's youth are eager to learn from the West, but are not in any way embarrassed about being Indian, e.g., MTV survives only because it has Indianized itself. They're willing to come together on non-sectarian issues for the larger good. Notice the immense passion that the issue of corruption has aroused. They're far more eclectic in their reading habits than their parents ever were. Books on subjects ranging from call centres to religious philosophies have found their way to mass acceptance and success. Most of the authors in recent bestseller charts are Indians. But the youth are not closed-minded. When a foreigner like Paulo Coelho comes along with philosophies which inspire them, they pick that up too.

The youth of today are the children of the liberalization era. They will come of age and one day make us proud. They will make India a great nation once again. We have many seemingly insurmountable challenges. With the right attitude, we'll crack them all!

I was asked by *Outlook* magazine to give my message to the youth. I'm not sure if I'm worthy of it. But I will share a line of encouragement. This is an immortal statement from *my* early youth; it is from a movie called *Star Wars*, which is remembered to this day: May the force be with you! Actually, maybe we can Indianize that a bit. May Shakti be with you!

First published in *Outlook*, 2011

Vedic Learning

It's wise to resist the temptation to only read articles that align with our worldview. Opening our minds to all shades of opinion can be enlightening. We might otherwise find ourselves inhabiting 'echo chambers', leading to an accentuating divisiveness in society, in an interesting play-out of Aristotle's law of excluded middle.

One such discourse that is heavily politicized, making rational discussion impossible, is the study of Vedic knowledge: Vedic science, mathematics, liberal philosophies, literature, politics, economics, ethics, etc. Interestingly, foreign universities have full-fledged departments dedicated to these subjects; but most of them encapsulate a superficial understanding. Departments in Indian universities on these subjects are woefully understaffed and under-resourced.

Articles and vocal opinions express dire warnings of the dangers of Vedic studies; the fear is this will lead to 'saffronization'. An earnest friend remarked that this 'right-wing pride-building project of Vedic studies will lead to extremism and hatred; and remember, pride comes before a fall.'

Reducing Vedic studies to a purely 'right-wing project' is an affront to the wealth of wisdom from our past. Our Vedic heritage is not the preserve of 'right-wing Hindus' alone; it belongs to everyone in the Indian subcontinent. Genetic studies have revealed that most people within the subcontinent carry combinations of the Ancestral-North-Indian (ANI) and the Ancestral-South-Indian (ASI) genetic groups. These groups have inhabited the subcontinent for at least 6,000 years, if not more, heavily intermingling in the ancient past.

Contrary to popular belief in the 'racial distinctness' of North Indians and South Indians, practically all north Indians have some proportion of ASI, and South Indians some proportion of ANI, in their gene pool. That means almost all groups in the Indian subcontinent today have descended from the ancient Vedic people. This holds true across religions, languages, castes and even national boundaries. It would be wrong for any group to claim exclusive rights over Vedic knowledge; it is the subcontinent's heritage. Studying it is not a 'right-wing' project. It concerns us all.

Let's talk about this issue of 'pride'. It is contended that the study of Vedic life will generate pride within us, and that this is inappropriate, even dangerous. We should instead focus on the future. Indeed obsessing about our past and ignoring our future is immature. However, should we swing to the other extreme and ignore our past completely? Is pride such an all-encompassing negative quality?

It is said that pride comes before a fall. But one cannot fall if one hasn't risen to begin with, or is weighed down by timidity. There are stages in the acquisition of pride. It begins with confidence and self-respect which help you succeed. Over time, this may transform into pride and regrettably, even arrogance; that's when you fall.

All great leaders and nations have understood the role that self-respect plays in achieving success. They build myths about their societies and their past. Many a time, these myths are not based on known facts. However, as long as the people believe in them, society moves forward, powered by confidence. The Anglo-Saxons of the US and Great Britain appropriated many of the Greek myths, even though they were a different ethnic group; they differed culturally as well, as the ancient Greeks weren't Christian but 'pagan'.

The Aryan invasion theory (now believed by many to be a work of fiction) was proposed by the Germans and British with similar motives. The Germans wanted to appropriate a great past by arrogating to themselves the Vedic way of life. Remember, they couldn't claim the Roman heritage since history has recorded that Germanic tribes destroyed the Roman Empire. The Aryan myth worked well for the British as well, to be used against the colonized Indians living under their yoke. A psychologically powerful way to subdue them was to convince them that what they thought was their greatest achievement, the Vedic way of life, was actually the gift of invading 'white men'. Destroyed pride made for a compliant populace.

Pride is good. All great nations understood this. In our case, we need not resort to fiction to instil pride in ourselves. The Vedic people *were* our ancestors. We should have justifiable pride in their achievements and tap into the vast knowledge they left behind. As for the risk of arrogance, which may follow pride, those pitfalls can be avoided with help from our rich treasure-trove of archetypes. Concepts like integral unity and oneness teach us that it is in our own interest to guard against hatred for the other and the arrogance it leads to. But for now, it is important to build our pride; for it is the fuel that will help us build our nation.

Let's study the works of our Vedic ancestors. Let us harness our past, look to the future with confidence and create, once again, a great, genuinely liberal, wealthy and just society.

First published in *The Times of India,* September 2014

Wajid Ali Shah: The Virtuoso

The British Raj has no doubt bequeathed a few assets—both tangible and intangible—not least notably the language in which I pen my thoughts here. Nevertheless, one must also acknowledge that it had many deleterious consequences. Estimates vary, but between forty to sixty million Indians died in famines callously engineered by British Raj administrators; history records that famines were relatively rare prior to British rule.

Famines may well be behind us, but other insidious effects of colonialism continue to bedevil us. George Orwell had said, 'The most effective way to destroy a people is to deny and obliterate their own understanding of their history.' Sadly, colonial historical perspectives prevail due to ideological leanings of many post-Independence Indian historians. I have written in this book (also see The Myth of the Aryan invasion theory, page 139) about the fictitious 'Aryan invasion theory' or AIT.

In this piece, I shall focus on a subject brought to my attention by my brother-in-law, Himanshu, an aficionado of Indian classical music. I bring to your notice the image constructed by the British of Nawab Wajid Ali Shah. Sadly, many of us (except those belonging to Lucknow) have either forgotten this Muslim ruler of Awadh or harbour the British impression of him as a decadent, cross-dressing oddity. This is a tragic humiliation of a great son of India.

Ancient Indian performing arts had declined drastically in north India in the latter part of the Mughal period, for various reasons. Rapacious tax and cultural policies of subsequent British rule hastened this decline.

The foundation of Hindustani and Carnatic music goes back many millennia, embedded as it is in the *Sama Veda*. The frameworks of the ragas, ancient in conception, are grounded in the precision and harmony of mathematics. However, great experimentation is allowed within this broad framework. The same raga, performed by different artists, exhibits variations. Amazingly, the same performer interprets a raga differently at different points in time! Each performance of Indian classical music is, hence, unique. The *guru-shishya parampara* (the teacher-pupil tradition) is a crucial factor in keeping this tradition alive and vibrant; this had tragically broken down due to the absence of nurturing patronage at the time.

And when this heritage was gasping for sustenance, the nawab revived it with his abundant munificence. He may not have been much of a warrior. But not every great ruler need seek validation through exploits on the battlefield. Many have attained greatness through contributions to the cultural legacy of their land. Wajid Ali Shah lavished money on performers, musicians, playwrights, poets and dancers. They flocked to Lucknow, his glittering capital. Many declining *gharanas* ('families'/places where a musical style originated) were revived. Intense artistic intermingling produced new ragas as well as other innovative expressions. A new version of *thumri*, which is mostly inspired by Lord Krishna, was reportedly an innovation of the nawab's court, even as greats like Ustads Basit Khan, Pyar Khan and Jaffer Khan breathed the eclectic air around the great ruler. Kathak, a charming Indian dance form, was revived under his guidance as patronage was lavished upon the brilliant Durga Prasadji and Thakur Prasadji.

Wajid Ali Shah himself was an artiste of merit. He wrote forty works: poems, prose and plays. He composed many new ragas such as the jogi and juhi. It has been held that he was, despite his girth, an accomplished dancer.

Reading the works of historian G.D. Bhatnagar will elucidate that British tales of his 'wanton', alcoholic ways were patently untrue and, in all probability, was false propaganda to justify the takeover of Awadh, a fabulously rich kingdom of the time. Wajid Ali Shah was a devout Muslim. He also honoured the Hindu God Lord Krishna. He authored some fascinating plays on *Krishna Ras Lila* and is believed to have himself acted in them on occasion. He wrote *Babul Mora Naihar*, the haunting song describing a bride's tearful farewell from her beloved father's home. Apocryphally, it served as a metaphor for the nawab's own banishment from his treasured Lucknow.

Historians have recorded some of his wise administrative reforms, stymied though he was by the British Resident, General Sleeman, who played a role in the defamation of Wajid Ali Shah. G.D. Bhatnagar has noted that for all the accusations of decadence and financial profligacy by the British, the nawab did not ask for a loan from any private banker or from the colonial masters to pay off any arrears. After his ouster, he did not leave behind any large arrears or debt. Awadh was, indeed, a fabulously affluent kingdom, which is why the British annexed this 'Queen province of India'.

Tell me now, should we or should we not remember this man as a great son of India who kept a significant aspect of our culture alive at a terribly difficult time?

You know what I'm going to do? I will curl up and listen to Raga Malkauns once again. And as I listen to the strains of this raga dedicated to my God, Lord Shiva, I will thank a long-dead, misunderstood Muslim from Lucknow, who played a remarkable role in ensuring that a delicate, beautiful facet of our heritage remained alive.

First published in *The Times of India,* March 2016

Where the Speech Is Without Fear...

Imprinted in the minds of Indians are Pandit Jawaharlal Nehru's words delivered at the stroke of midnight on that most important day: when the soul of a nation, long suppressed, found utterance. Every Indian heart, in that precious moment, must have longed for its beloved India to soon sprout wings and fly. I find myself wondering today, what was the point of it all, if the wings were used to fly in the wrong direction? One that is not attuned to our innate culture? We made one such unfortunate turn early in our post-independent history.

Freedom-loving liberals among us must remember and hang our heads in shame at the regrettable turn we took on 10 May 1951. That was the day Pandit Jawaharlal Nehru piloted the First Amendment to the Indian Constitution (which was passed into law within the next few weeks). Among other restrictions on our fundamental rights, this also restricted freedom of expression.

It is believed that this was in response to the Supreme Court judgment in 1950 on the 'Romesh Thapar vs The State of Madras' case, through which the ban on Romesh Thapar's magazine (a Marxist journal called *Cross Roads*), was lifted. Many lawyers opine that in effect, the Supreme Court had recognized unfettered freedom of expression as compliant with our original Constitution; just like in the case of the United States, and in fact, one that was far better than in Europe at the time. Legal luminaries also hold that since unfettered freedom of expression would have established itself as a fundamental right, the illiberal IPC section 295(a), a gift bequeathed by the British Raj, using which many books have been banned, would be overridden.

Why did the Nehru government pass the First Amendment? Critics of Prime Minister Nehru will hold this as proof that he was not a classical liberal (defined as one who defends political and economic freedoms for all). Supporters of Prime Minister Nehru will say that he had to ensure unity of purpose in the first few years of Independent India to stabilize our country; and some freedoms were a small price to pay in the interest of a superior need for order. I'll let historians pass judgements on this issue.

I merely offer my humble take on the events that transpired at the time; an observation that is based on my beliefs on freedom of expression. And this is not just as a liberal, but also as an inheritor of a culture that has a proud, millennia-long tradition of ideational freedom.

Freedom of expression is, frankly, the most Indian of values; one that was staunchly defended by Lord Brahma Himself in the *Natya Shastra*. Ancient India offered the freedom to create, and encouraged various versions of the holiest of epics like the Ramayan and Mahabharat; and all versions, some even unorthodox, were celebrated. In fact one could even be an atheist in ancient India, like the Charvaks were, and none would cast them outside the folds of philosophical study, leave alone single them out for spiteful violence owing to their being 'ungodly'. One could practice out-of-the-ordinary rituals, like the Aghoras who performed ritual sex. None would ban their practices so long as they didn't hurt another, unlike in modern India. Everybody exercised the right to their own truth; in keeping with the spirit of the Rig Vedic maxim: *Ekam sat vipra bahuda vadanti*. Truth is one, but the wise men speak (or know) it as many.

I would ask for only two restrictions to be placed on freedom of expression: if it is exercised to suppress the freedom of expression of another. Or if it is used to *directly* call for violence. In every other case, absolute and unfettered freedom of expression should be allowed to prevail in a civilized society. Every banned book should be unbanned. Every argument, however troubling or even 'offensive' it may be, should be allowed expression. In this context, it may be apt to quote Sigmund Freud, who said that the first human who hurled an insult instead of a stone, was the founder of civilization.

All of us who count ourselves among the liberals, and are proud Indians, must ask for the First Amendment to be repealed. Moreover, we must not practice the hypocritical freedom of expression that the Westerners practice, wherein views at variance with the prevailing orthodoxy are suppressed; not through violence, but by ensuring that one is excluded from participation in various public forums or one's works are not published, e.g., the gagging and outcasting of Ayaan Hirsi Ali. I disagree with many things Ms Ali says, but we must defend the right to speak of even those whose views are deeply troubling; provided that there is no direct call for violence.

Stopping the free flow of ideas is against India's innate culture and heritage. We are not in any sense being 'Western' if we ask for unfettered freedom of expression. In fact, we are being *very* Indian.

Furthermore, as our ancestors knew thousands of years ago, freedom of expression is the foundation of a liberal and decent society. As the *Rig Veda* says: 'In Speech is enshrined blessed glory, is enshrined Mother Lakshmi Herself.'

First published in *The Times of India,* November 2014

A Calm Rebellion

To be honest, it is quite incredible that someone with my background is standing here, speaking to you as a supposedly successful author. To begin with, I was not 'born right' for the world of English-language publishing in India. Why is that? I don't come from an upper class background, with linkages and connections to the elite slab of Indian society. Moreover, I spoke, and continue to speak with my parents in Hindi. Therefore, I think in a mix of Hindi and English, which constrains my English language abilities, as compared to the Indian upper class. Also, my higher education was not right for the English-language publishing industry in India. I graduated in mathematics, got an MBA from IIM Kolkata, after which I became a banker. There are too many bankers in the world; on this stage as well! And I was told that mathematics and an MBA was not that bad a qualification. Or more specifically, not bad at all for banking. But for the English-language publishing industry, perhaps not. Even today, MBAs are probably considered upwardly mobile newbies who're not connected to the cultural sphere. Furthermore, the most important reason why I shouldn't have been a successful author, is that I had no prior experience or training in writing. I had written absolutely no fiction before *The Immortals of Meluha*.

I had dabbled in some poetry in my college days; but they were amateur attempts. The only person who liked them was my wife, who at that time was my girlfriend. So I didn't have the right background, education or experience to be a writer. And yet I somehow made it. I can try and claim credit for this success, but honestly that would be a lie. This may sound strange to some of you, but I believe it is the blessings of Lord Shiva because He ensured that I was in the right place at the right time.

There is a mood of rebellion in India today. An outsider banging on the doors finds support. And I happen to be that lucky outsider who wrote a book on the original outsider God. The God of the rebels. The anti-elite God, Lord Shiva. So I am, frankly, a lucky beneficiary of this mood of rebellion, of anger against the elite, that is prevalent in the country today. So I should be in favour of this mood of rebellion, right? I should be saying yes, go on, be rebellious, man. Be a rebel without a cause.

But I am going to say something slightly different here—that maybe, we need to tone down this rebelliousness a bit. I know we are Indians, we are emotional, and we don't do the 'keep calm' thing, but maybe we should give it a try. Why am I suggesting that? Anger has its uses, after all. But if we don't maintain our sense of calm at such times, we may lose focus on the real issues. Resultantly, we can dissipate our anger on issues where we should not be getting so angry. Let me explain this through three key issues which anger us today in India.

The first is corruption. There are those who maintain that as a civilization, we are inherently corrupt. After all, they say, we even bribe our Gods for seeking blessings and answers to our prayers. So, it is claimed, that we are, basically, a corrupt culture and nothing can be done about it. There is a lot of anger about this issue in India, right? The point I'd like to make is, we are not very different from others at this stage of our development. Almost every country has experienced a period of massive and all-pervasive corruption: the UK in the eighteenth and nineteenth century, the US in the early nineteenth and twentieth century, and China right now. Interestingly, this phase of massive corruption was usually accompanied by an initial thrust of breakneck economic growth. These countries managed to tackle corruption over time, and bring it down to a reasonable level. China is on the journey, albeit ahead of us. Which means that we can do it as well. It's a phase, perhaps owing to the fast economic growth that we are experiencing. For example, the telecom scam did not happen in an earlier era, since spectrum had no value when we were poor; a thriving telecom industry opened up an opportunity. The criminals involved in this corruption must be brought to book through the due process of law. There are many other examples of corruption, and if we want to get rid of them, we must follow the due process of the law. However, too much anger, fuelled by a desire for mob justice, may actually end up harming our own country.

I am not denying that attacking corruption is important. But I am sure all of us will agree that fast economic growth is even more important. We need to generate enough jobs for the army of youth in India. There are roughly thirteen million youth who join the workforce every year. If we don't create jobs for them, our demographic dividend will very quickly become a demographic curse, resulting in violence and chaos. So we must attack corruption, but not with a sense of mob justice, which will derail our economy.

There is a second issue I'd like to draw your attention to: communal violence. This is something that troubles us all. In this context, terms like 'genocide' are actually thrown around with little caution, I think (also see Religious Violence in India, page 81). There have been sixty major incidents of religious violence in India (incidents in which more than five people were killed) in the last fifty years. Five of these were major riots, where more than a thousand were killed. Let me reiterate that even a single death in religious violence is unacceptable. Can our police and civil administration systems be tightened to ensure that these riots don't occur? Of course. Can our judicial system and courts be improved so that the perpetrators are quickly brought to justice? Yes, most certainly. But if we step back and think calmly, can any of these riots be classified as genocides? Frankly, no. A genocide is when millions or even lakhs are killed. If we examine the causes of unnatural deaths in India, religious violence is actually a very minuscule portion. No doubt, we must tackle this issue of religious violence head-on; but is this deserving of the levels of anger that it incites in our civil society? Religious intolerance is a problem facing the human species as a whole and we need to address it. But I don't think India is poised to destroy itself in an orgy of religious violence. We have crossed that bridge. Let's diffuse the anger on this issue.

My third point concerns an issue that I suggest should generate a healthy dose of anger. If you're looking for a genocide in our country today, it's happening with the women of India. In the last twenty years, ten million female foetuses have been illegally aborted. Ten million girls have been killed in the womb in the last two decades! This is genocide. And we are simply not angry enough about it. To say that China is worse than us is not an excuse. In fact, we can learn from another neighbour on this issue—Bangladesh, which has shown among the fastest improvements in social indicators in the history of humanity, right up there with the Meiji-restoration era in Japan. And they have achieved this while still being abysmally poor. The secret of their success is women's empowerment. That's the magic pill with which they got it right. Repeated surveys from developing countries have shown that if you lend money to the women instead of men, it results in better social outcomes. Women tend to spend that money sensibly—on better nutrition for the family or education for the children. The day we empower our women, we build a better society.

Now, in our present mood of anger and rebellion, we'd like to blame the government for this problem. We somehow expect it to resolve the issue of women's oppression in India. Frankly, it would do us a whole lot of good if the national and state governments focussed on governance issues like the lack of infrastructure and fiscal deficit. If one were to follow the model of the traditional Chanakyan state, social issues should be left to the society. In any case, the problem is caused by the society itself and not the government. So, the onus for solving such a problem should not rest with the police or any other arm of the government; it's the society which should step in and correct it. All of us need to fight this good fight in our own little corners of the world. For instance, if your father is ill-treating your mother, you need to rebel. If you find a daughter-in-law being oppressed by the mother-in-law (or the other way round, since that is also, sadly, common), you need to stand up for the rights of the woman. If your household help is not able to educate his/her daughter, you need to help them fulfil their duty. You need to deal with this issue in every sphere of your life and not just within your home. Everywhere, all of us have to fight this fight. That's the only way to bring about change. This is an issue that we *must* get angry about.

Our ancient scriptures state that even Gods abandon a land where women are not respected. So, I believe that fighting on this issue is our patriotic duty.

One of the things I have learnt is that sometimes it's useful to keep a calm head and carefully pick the issues that urgently require our rebelliousness and anger.

At all other times, the 'keep calm' thing is not such a bad idea.

UN Young Changemakers Conclave, June 2014

Rebuilding a Temple. Fulfilling an Ancient Call of Duty.

As the reconstruction of the Ram Janmabhoomi temple begins in Ayodhya, I am drawn to another piece of news, half a world away. The Hagia Sophia Museum in Istanbul has just been converted back into a mosque. It is the decision of their highest court of law, undoing the earlier decision of the secularizing Kemal Ataturk (the founder of the Republic of Turkey) in 1935. I had travelled to Turkey two years ago and could sense that this was an emotional subject for the Turks. I saw their yearning to exclusively pray once again at their holy place, without being surrounded by tourists (prayers had been allowed in the museum in the recent past). From the perspective of most of the Turks, the decision was understandably fair. However, I also understand the pain of the Greek Orthodox Christians. Pope Francis said that he was 'deeply pained'. For the Hagia Sophia was once a church. In 1453, the Turks conquered Constantinople (the centre of the Greek Orthodox Church for a millennium), erased its very name, birthed the city of Istanbul, and converted the Hagia Sophia church into a mosque. Don't the Greek Orthodox Christians yearn to pray there as well? And many Roman Catholic Christians too, for the Hagia Sophia was also a Roman Catholic church once, albeit briefly? But I take my brooding further. The mother of all ironies is that no one feels the pain of the pagan temple upon the foundations of which the Hagia Sophia itself was constructed over 1,500 years ago. So, are we being told that historical wrongs go this far in time? No further? Why not? Because almost no pagan survives in Europe to feel the pain and hurt from the historical wrong.

Pagan is a pejorative word, used to describe those who are not Abrahamic, i.e., those who do not follow any one of Judaism, Christianity or Islam. I embrace this 'deprecatory' term with responsibility. It is forgotten that practically the entire ancient world was 'pagan' once; idol-worshipping, Goddess-worshipping, nature-worshipping people who were comfortable with multiple Truths and forms of the Divine; even atheists were included. Many would follow multiple 'religions', something unthinkable in strict Abrahamism. All these cultures were wiped out, most of them violently. Judaism was rarely an imperialist religion. But proselytizing Christians and Muslims inflicted unprecedented genocidal violence upon pagans, spoken poignantly of in Katherine Nixey's *The Darkening Age*, among many other books. But it must be strongly asserted that not all Christians or Muslims were oppressors of the pagans. There were a few groups that carried out this violence: most prominently, European Christians and Turkic Muslims. This violent expansionist urge was absent, for instance, in the African Christians and Indonesian Muslims. And of course, very obviously, modern Europeans and Turks have nothing to do with what their ancestors did.

Why is this historical sweep important for us Indians? Because we are among the few 'pagan cultures' to have survived. We are the only pre-Bronze-Age civilization with a living, continuous culture (China, though a 'pagan culture', is not pre-Bronze Age).

And we suffered, as all pagans did. There were repeated invasions through the second millennium CE, first by various Turkic tribes, and then by European colonialists. Establishment Indian historians from the old elite refer to the Turkic invasions as Islamic invasions, but they do not call the European conquest the Christian conquest. This reflects their bias. I believe that they should be referred to as Turkic and European invasions; for the foreign invaders had nothing to do with Indian Muslims or Indian Christians. But the foreigners were, self-declaredly, steeped in a deeply iconoclastic doctrine. Thousands of temples were destroyed, and mosques or churches were built on the same ground, sometimes reusing the rubble of the destroyed temple. Sita Ram Goel has recorded many instances in his seminal book *Hindu Temples: What Happened to Them*. Tens of universities were burnt to the ground. Many tens of millions of people were massacred over the centuries. American historian Will Durant had said that the Turkic invasions of India were the most brutal in human history. But the Europeans were no less brutal, as the true history of the Goa Inquisition shows... Notwithstanding, what happened to us was not unique. It happened to almost every single ancient and classical culture in the world. What is unique is that we survived. How and why? One of the main reasons is that our ancestors did not surrender.

The Sun Temple in Multan was the first major ancient Indian temple to be attacked by a foreign invader in the early eighth century CE. Thereafter, thousands of Hindu and Jain temples, Buddhist viharas and Sikh gurudwaras were destroyed by invaders, including the Holiest of Holies like the Ram Janmabhoomiji temple in Ayodhya, the Vishwanathji temple in Kashi and the Keshav Devaji temple in Mathura. Some say that pagan invaders also destroyed places of worship at times, most notably the

Romans, who destroyed the Jewish Temple at Jerusalem. But history records that these were rare, and not theologically driven. Equivalences drawn look belaboured and disingenuous, in the face of the overwhelming preponderance of numbers in favour of the iconoclasts. The pagan attacks on other places of worship are less than minuscule when compared to the scale of what the pre-modern Europeans, Turks, and few other invading groups did in the last one and a half millennia. A gruesome murder, heinous as it may be, cannot be equated with wholesale massacre. It has been theorized by some historians that these barbaric foreign invaders attacked temples only for their riches, and the destruction was an unintended consequence. If that were true, mere looting would have sufficed, and destroying the temples/viharas and converting them into mosques or churches would not have been necessary. And what monetary gain could be made by destroying universities? The brutal Turk Bakthiyar Khilji burned so many books in Nalanda university, that the fire burned for many months. The conquerors themselves proudly recorded their destructive acts, along with their iconoclastic motives, in texts such as Baburnama and Tarikh-i-Firishta, among many others.

Indian kings and queens took some time to understand the nature and character of these invaders. Some discovered the hard way that classical codes of chivalrous honour in battle were outdated against such foes (Prithviraj Chauhan, for example). Many others fought heroically and won (King Suheldev, Chhatrapati Shivaji Maharaj, Lachit Borphukan, Maharaja Ranjit Singh, King Marthanda Varma, Queen Abbakka, among many others). Many fought hard and lost (Raja Dahir of Sind, Hindushahi Maharaja Jayapala of Kabul, among others). Some won, some lost, many died in battle, but our ancestors never surrendered. And because they never surrendered, they were the only ones among all pre-Bronze-Age pagans who succeeded in protecting that which is most precious: their way of life.

I am reminded of these wonderful lines, ironically written by the bugbear of a few in India, Baron Macaulay, 'And how can man die better/ Than facing fearful odds/ For the ashes of his fathers/ And the temples of his Gods.'

Our ancestors did the dying. It is up to us to do the rebuilding.

As we rebuild, we must remember to not dishonour our ancients or their way of life. We must act with dharma. We must speak the truth of what happened to our civilization but without engendering hatred. We must act, but with calm collective resolve, not with insecure aggression. We must understand that Indian Muslims and Christians of today, have nothing to do with what the pre-modern Europeans, Turks, and other foreign invaders did. We must rebuild our temples and viharas as one people. With mutual respect and love. Inclusion. We must recreate them as not just places of worship, but also as centres of knowledge and social cohesion, as they were in ancient times. We must not stop with the Ram Janmabhoomi temple. We have much more to rebuild; the Martand Sun temple in Kashmir and the University of Vikramshila in Bihar, for instance.

Rebuilding is a civilizational responsibility we owe to ourselves—and more significantly, to our ancestors, as well as to future generations. It is a statement to the world. That we will not die. We are *sanatan*. We are eternal. And most importantly, we are united. All 1.3 billion of us.

Jai Shri Ram. Jai Maa Bharati.

First published in The Print, April 2020

Musings

Why I Write

One of my identities today is that of an author. Six months ago, my professional identity was different. I was a banker: a traditional MBA, *suited-booted*, jargon-spewing finance type. It's been a long and strange journey: from finance to writing fiction. Some of you might say, long? Ok, I concede that point! But, strange? Well, there are reasons for it, so if you allow me…

The first reason is that my books are historical; they are set in the India of 4,000 years ago. The strange part is that I didn't study history at a higher level; I graduated in mathematics. Some may say I am a masochist for doing so! The second oddity is that I write fiction books. But before my first book, *The Immortals of Meluha*, was released last year, I had written absolutely no fiction in my life. Not even a short story in school; except for some really terrible poetry in my college days, which no one liked. The only one who indulged me and liked my poems was my girlfriend; today she is my wife. The third strange thing is that I have written about the adventures of the Hindu God, Lord Shiva. My books are based on the premise that Lord Shiva was a historical man who lived 4,000 years ago and through His grand adventures and karma, He became God. So, well, I've written on a Hindu God. But I was an atheist till eight-nine years ago. Today, of course, I am a very devoted Shiva worshipper. But in my early youth, I did not feel the need to even enter temples. It's been a really long and strange journey. So how did it happen? How did someone like me, an atheist, graduate in mathematics, who was devoid of any imagination, actually end up writing historical fiction on a God?

I have a theory. I believe my books are a blessing. And my soul prepared me, over decades, to receive this blessing. Moreover, it was done without my conscious knowledge. How did this happen? Let me first cover the history 'section'. For as long as I can remember, extending to my childhood, I was always attracted to the subject of history. Why? I don't know. Now, I'm a pragmatic guy. You know the banker profile, right? I knew that being a historian was not a well-paying career option; at least not in the early 1990s when I was growing up. And I don't have any family wealth to fall back on. So I did an MBA and joined the exciting world of banking. But life needn't be an 'either or'. One can always find the time to indulge a passion. So I continued to voraciously read several books on history. Not because it would help me in my career or get me good grades, but just because I was happy with such a book in my hand.

Now the other oddity: writing. An idea entered my mind around eight-nine years ago; I felt the need to write about it. But I was unsure. My family actively encouraged me. They said to me, 'Yaar, this sounds good, write it down.' And I felt compelled to listen to them. Not because I always do what my family asks me to. The real reason was that I was deeply unhappy when I was not working on my book. I was in a high-pressure job at that point in time. I worked in the banking sector; we were busy destroying the financial world; it takes a lot of time and effort, right? I simply did not have the time to write a book. Being the pragmatic guy, I did a logical thing; I banished every 'time-wasting activity' from my life and restricted myself to only three things: doing my job, spending time with my family and writing my book. I stopped watching TV, partying, even exercising. But I was still unable to find enough time to write. Essentially, I was writing only on Sundays.

Then my wife had an insight. She pointed out that I was wasting two-three hours every day on my office commute. This was Mumbai, and I was driving to and from work every day. Need I say more? She suggested that we employ a driver. Drivers were easily available those days, and that was the best 5,000 rupees per month that I ever invested. Soon I was writing my book in the backseat of my car. It took me four-five years, but the book eventually emerged.

I have been told that there are some authors in this room. It might appear to non-authors that once the book is written, the journey is over. Actually no, not by a long shot! You have to get it published, which is an entirely new story by itself. My agent and I made innumerable rounds in the corridors of the Indian publishing industry. I was warned that the Indian publishing space is fractious. Collect eleven publishers in one room and you are likely to end up with twelve opinions! But I was in for a surprise; on my book there was rare unanimity.

Every single publisher who read my book thought there was no way it would work. Everyone rejected it. How many? Quite frankly, I stopped counting after twenty. This was not going anywhere. A few publishers were kind enough to give me reasons for rejecting my book. One suggested I would alienate every single reader segment with my book. I said: 'Okay, how?' He said to me, 'Look, you are writing on religion which the youth aren't really interested in. You have your own take on religion, you're unorthodox, and the elders will not like it. Finally, you're insisting on writing in modern, easy English which means the literati won't like it. So who in God's name are you writing for? Which reader segment are you planning to sell it to?' I said, 'Look, I didn't do market research before writing my book, I just wrote the book.' Anyway, the sum and substance was that my book was rejected by everyone.

Now, my wife is this lovely, supportive woman. I think she was so stunned that a creatively-challenged person like me had actually written a book that she felt compelled to support it in every way possible. She suggested that if need be, we would cut back on some expenses, but would publish the book ourselves. Even if that meant that we would only be able to print the book and distribute it free of cost to our family and friends. I said: 'Okay, great, thanks sweetheart. 'But I had another surprise in store for me. My agent, my long suffering agent, who had sent my book to every publisher and had had the door slammed shut on his face, was also moved by my belief in the book. He offered to invest in printing if I would invest in the marketing. I said: 'Okay, great, thanks man.' Through this providential partnership, my book, *The Immortals of Meluha*, was launched in March 2010. Believe me, I had absolutely no expectations, but the book actually hit the bestsellers chart within the first week of its launch.

So what's the point of my speech? Is it that if you follow your soul's advice, you will certainly find success? That may be true but this point has been made by many people, by those who are wiser than I am, in language that's more poetic than mine. My point is entirely different. It is that if you listen to your soul and discover your life's purpose, success or failure actually ceases to matter. And that is the wonderful place I discovered.

While I was in banking, if I had been asked to give up all my trappings of success: the glass-walled cabin, the bonus, the salary, the personal assistant, the senior management rank … and then asked if I would be equally happy in my banking career, the honest answer would be no, I would not be. Success was a prerequisite for me liking my banking career. There were times when I didn't get the promotion I thought I deserved, or the bonus I got was less than what I should have got. At such times, it was not just my motivation that nosedived but also my personal happiness. But in my writing career, the story is completely different. If someone had told me that my books would be super flops; that *The Immortals of Meluha* and *The Secret of the Nagas* would not sell the way they have, that they would only sell twenty-five copies each; would I still be happy? The honest answer is yes. Success or failure truly became irrelevant in my writing career. Even at the time when my book was being rejected by every publisher, left, right and centre, not for a moment did I think that I had wasted my time in writing this book. Even when it seemed that my book would never get published, I'd already started writing my second book. I know that had my books failed, I'd still be working in the banking sector. But I would also be writing, even if my books remained in my laptop. Even if the only people reading my books would be my long-suffering family; I would continue to write. And that is a wonderful place to be in. For then the journey itself becomes a thing of joy and the destination is immaterial.

My mother, brilliant woman that she is, had once told me that if you find that your work itself gives you pleasure, and that failure doesn't fill your heart with sadness, and success doesn't fill your mind with pride, then you know you are working in consonance with your soul's purpose, your own *swadharma*. I am in that wonderful place. Whenever I write or do anything associated with my books, there is a deep, profound and unrelenting happiness that I feel within. To me, that's life's greatest blessing. And that blessing is available to every single one of us; all we have to do is listen to the voice of our soul and find our life's true purpose. Thank you.

Ink Talks, Jaipur, 2012

Science, Spirituality and My Son Neel

My wife, my four-year-old son Neel and I had gone to Switzerland in 2013. We visited many places which held little interest for my wife and me, but which Neel loved: transport museums, bear parks and more toy-train rides than we'd care to remember. His joyful laughter, however, made them tolerable for us.

Now there was one place which I desperately wanted to visit as well: CERN (European Organization for Nuclear Research), Geneva. This was for various reasons. I am a lover of science and regularly read many scientific papers. Also, CERN had installed a beautiful idol of Lord Shiva in His Nataraj form, celebrating the cosmic dance of my God. A visit to CERN was like a pilgrimage for me. Furthermore, I have always been intrigued by the Standard Model, having read on the subject and spent some memorable evenings over extended discussions on it, with a cousin who's a scientist in Pune. I'm sure you are aware that what we learnt about 'matter' in school was incomplete. All constituents of matter are actually classified as constructs of fermions (named after the Italian physicist Enrico Fermi) and bosons (named after our very own S.N. Bose). Also, there are four fundamental forces of interaction in the universe: electromagnetic, gravitation, weak-interaction and strong-interaction. The 'strong-interaction' force is most intriguing. Counter-intuitively, this force of attraction *does not weaken* as you pull particles apart. There is almost a spiritual lesson in this. A visit to CERN was a great opportunity to explore this idea further. What I didn't realize was that my son could have taught me better. How?

Well, Neel did not want to visit CERN. It was only natural. He was a four-year-old who was more interested in dinosaurs and nature. He is yet to discover his passion for particle physics! So we'd made a plan that my wife would go to a park with him while I would head off alone on my 'science excursion'. However, on the morning of the visit, he decided to come along to CERN. I was genuinely surprised. So was my wife, Preeti. Therefore, she asked him: 'Why do you want to go to CERN?'

Neel's answer was simple: 'I want to go because dad wants to go.'

The 'strong-interaction' force does not weaken when particles are pulled apart. There is a spiritual lesson in that. My son Neel taught me. And it was such a moving lesson, that it brought tears to my eyes.

First published in *Hindustan Times*, 2013

The Three Wise Women

All who have read my books would know that I normally take a 1,00,000 words and 400 pages to make my point! Notwithstanding that, I was asked by *Femina* to write the story of my life, with a special emphasis on the influence that women have had upon it. And I had to do this in a 1,000 words. Have mercy!

I decided therefore to restrict myself to three incidents, which had deeply impacted me. Needless to say, all of them involved the women in my life.

The first incident harks back to my childhood, when I was around eight years old. We lived in a compact company colony called Kansbahal, near Rourkela in Orissa; my father was employed by Larsen and Toubro at the time. My mother was a strict disciplinarian, while my father was the ever-indulgent parent. One evening, my twin brother Ashish and I decided to trot off to the colony club. We had asked Maa for permission, and she had said no, as we had not finished our homework. An hour later, when Paa returned from office, we asked him. And he of course, said yes. We happily took off, gallivanted through the evening and returned at night, in time for dinner; to a troubled environment. Paa was livid as he spoke to us severely; this being an unusual experience, we began to cry. We tried to assure him that we'd finish our homework immediately, before turning in. But he was angry about something else: how dare we ask him for permission to do anything at all, when Maa had already said no to it? He said that if one of the parents says no, that automatically means both have said no. You don't play games within the family. And that was a lesson I learnt well. You don't play games within the family; more importantly, that the mother and father are equals.

The second incident was actually the genesis of the Shiva Trilogy. A TV programme triggered a discussion in my family, which in turn led to a philosophical idea that occurred to me: what is evil? Does evil serve a purpose? In their love for me and against their better judgement—keeping in mind my rather incoherent attempts at poetry earlier—my family encouraged me to start penning my thoughts down on paper. But I was unsure. And I remember that my elder sister, Bhavna and my twin brother, Ashish had a conversation with me. Bhavnadi said to me, how will I know that I cannot do something unless I try it? I needn't necessarily write to impress others, but to sift through the thoughts in my own mind and communicate it to my family, who wouldn't judge me. So who cares about the quality of the writing? Just go ahead and write. That was another lesson I learnt: never hesitate to try something. Why let the fear of failure prevent you from attempting something new? And most importantly, if you are doing something for yourself, who the hell cares what the world thinks?

The third incident occurred around the launch of the second book of the Shiva Trilogy, *The Secret of the Nagas*. By God's grace, the first book of the Trilogy, *The Immortals of Meluha*, had done well. The pre-bookings for the second book gave me the confidence that this too could be a success. Until then, I was writing while still working at my job, which was as a senior management committee member at a life insurance company. I looked after the departments of marketing, products and service quality. It was a high-pressure job which kept me busy six days a week. To add to that, I was writing and promoting my books in whatever free time I had. Essentially, I was burning the candle at both ends. Something had to give.

But I was still unsure of leaving my job. This was despite the fact that my royalty cheque had grown to be more than my salary. I'm not from a very wealthy background and couldn't afford to be irresponsible with my career choices. Moreover, we had just been blessed with a child and my wife had taken a break from work to look after him.

Then my wife Preeti and my elder brother Anish had a talk with me. They explained to me that I was being too risk-averse by not committing myself to writing full-time. Anishda said that I shall always have the option of going back to banking. But this opportunity to make a career as a writer was a blessing. And if it worked, I would live the kind of life that I completely love: reading, writing, travelling and spending time with my family. Preeti said something beautiful to me: that besides my responsibilities to my family, I also had a responsibility to myself, to pursue my dreams, to give my life greater meaning. She said that most people don't get an opportunity like this. And I had been blessed with one. The real irresponsibility would be to not grab it wholly and completely.

So I resigned from my job. I also made sure that I left my office with good relations; just in case I needed to go back to my earlier life! But the lesson learnt was this: of course we have responsibilities towards our loved ones. But we also have responsibilities towards ourselves. We should never forget that.

I'm not suggesting that these are the only three turning points in my life, but they are significant ones. Life is not only about the destination but also the journey. Looking back, dwelling upon the 'little events', gives one a sense of perspective; and a firm direction in the journey that remains.

May Lord Shiva and the Holy Lake bless you on your own journey as well.

First published in *Femina*, 2014

A Patriotic Manifesto

I just finished reading Shashi Tharoor's superlative *An Era of Darkness*, a study of the monstrosity that the British Raj was. And I felt a familiar rage; one that I had experienced many years ago when I had read Will Durant's *The Case for India* or Mike Davis' *Late Victorian Holocausts*. And many other such books that have catalogued the crimes against humanity that the British colonialists had carried out. It is estimated that they killed nearly forty million Indians in man-made famines. They ran the biggest drug-smuggling business in the history of humanity, which devastated India and China. A commentator had correctly said that Queen Victoria was essentially a drug lord; like a turbo-charged Dawood Ibrahim with better headdress. There were many other crimes, too many to list in this short article.

But a question arose in my mind, alongside. The British did not conquer us by themselves; after all, there were too few of them. Many Indian soldiers conquered India for them. The British did not run their drug-smuggling businesses by themselves; many Indian (and Chinese) businessmen did the dirty work for them. General Dyer may have ordered the shooting of defenceless Indians at Jallianwala Bagh, but the soldiers who actually wielded the guns were largely from the Indian subcontinent. Winston

Churchill (a war criminal no different from Hitler) may have given the orders for events that led to the Bengal Famine in the early 1940s (death toll estimated to be 1.5 to four million), but the officers who implemented his orders were largely Indian.

Why didn't the Indians, who committed these crimes on their own people, rebel? Why didn't they say, 'I will not do this to my people?' The nauseating apologists for the British Raj (many of whom are Indians) will say that this is because we didn't think of ourselves as 'Indian' since we were not one country before the British arrived. This is nonsense.

India as a cultural and civilizational entity has existed for millennia. There are enough examples and documentation to prove this. You can read the books I have mentioned above to find some of them. And in any case, before the treaties of Westphalia in the seventeenth century, 'nations' did not exist as political units, but as cultural entities. In sixteenth-century England, if you were loyal to England rather than King Henry VIII, you would have been beheaded as a traitor. But the cultural concept of England existed at the time. Just like the cultural concept of India did.

So, were the Indian collaborators driven by personal greed? That may help us understand the motivations of the businessmen who supported the Raj; they did become fabulously rich. But does that explain the behaviour of the Indian soldiers who fought and died for the Raj? There cannot be greater selflessness than dying for someone else, right? Some allege that the Indians who fought and died for the British were largely lower castes who were rebelling against the injustices in their own society by allying with a foreign power. This flies in the face of facts. Most soldiers who joined the British Army and helped the British conquer India in the eighteenth and early nineteenth century were actually upper castes (*Side note*: This same category of soldiers were the ones who rebelled in 1857 in the First Indian War of Independence). Why then did these people work against their own country's interests?

A thought has occurred to me, which I would like to present for your consideration.

For most of known history, India has led the world in terms of wealth and GDP, as well as knowledge and science. Our ancestors made discoveries and inventions in various fields such as mathematics, medicine, metallurgy, navigation, astronomy, etc. But our greatest contribution was in the area of spirituality and philosophy. I think that, perhaps, one innovation in this area, when taken to its extreme, did not work out well for us.

And that philosophical innovation is *swadharma*. Or the modern English word used to describe it: purpose.

As a philosophical construct to help us live a fruitful life, finding purpose is certainly a good idea. At its simplest, the concept is this: that you must discover your purpose, your *swadharma*, and live it; for only then will you find true achievement and personal happiness. Of course, you must discover your purpose on your own, and not allow society to enforce their interpretation on you. The beauty of finding purpose is that if you live your life in sync with it, then success or failure ceases to matter. You experience nothing but joy. As I do, when I live according to my purpose, which is to write books exploring and understanding the culture and philosophies of the nation that I love: India.

But *swadharma*, taken to its extreme, can lead to unbridled individualism and selfishness. It can give rise to citizens who do not stop to consider the impact of their *swadharma*, their *purpose*, on others or even the society as a whole. They focus only on what they must do to realize their purpose. Today, some scientists are working on projects which could dramatically impact society in a negative manner. Such as, genetically modified designer babies. And yet, they choose to continue, for they see their purpose as the pure pursuit of science; and not its impact on society.

I believe that India, being the home of *swadharma*, had created many individuals lost in their own purpose alone. The impact of their *swadharma* on society did not concern them. This may help us understand the mindset of Indian soldiers during the British Raj, lost in their *swadharma* of being warriors, even if it meant dying for a foreign power. But not stopping to consider the impact of their actions on their own society.

The British understood our culture well. They used the *swadharma* of the martial people among Indians, and used our best against us, by giving them purpose. Through pomp, ceremonies and rituals.

A society made up of individuals who are solely focussed on living their purpose can get atomized. Ironically, the society itself may fail to mobilize to pursue its collective purpose.

Now, I am not suggesting that we ignore our *swadharma*. It is our duty to live our life in alignment with our purpose. But we must not forget our Rajya Dharma either. Rajya Dharma, the duty towards the nation, is not just the preserve of the leaders. Rajya Dharma must also be followed by common citizens, all of us who live in this great land of ours.

Put another way, patriotism is as important as your personal purpose.

Patriotism is a much abused word these days. Many quote Samuel Johnson out of context, who had said, 'Patriotism is the last refuge of the scoundrel.' Evidence suggests that Johnson was referring to false patriotism when he said this; and he did value true patriotism.

That is what I am proposing. True patriotism. Rajya Dharma. Deep and abiding love for our native land. Love towards all who live here. Constructive love, which allows us to question our leaders when we believe they are not working in our country's or state's interests. Love which encourages us to question our own fellow citizens on things which must be improved, for we want our land to be worthy of our ancestors.

To me, love for our land is non-negotiable. We have every right to dislike our government, but we cannot live in India and righteously exercise the right to hate our country. A nation is not built by those who hate it. It is built on the shoulders of those who love it.

Let's learn from the mistakes of Indians in the last few centuries. We must focus on our *swadharma*, our purpose. But we must not forget our Rajya Dharma, our duty to this great land of ours.

Bharat Mata ki Jai. Glory to Mother India.

First published in *The Telegraph*

Black Panther, Africa and India

The Hollywood blockbuster *Black Panther*, which has earned more than $1 billion globally, has had a good run in India. It has been the subject of a wave of analyses on its messaging for African-Americans and Africa (sub-Saharan Africa in particular). Are there inherent lessons for India as well? I think so.

In *Black Panther*, M'Baku, the leader of the Jabari tribe (played by Winston Duke), says 'Glory to Hanuman' (though inexplicably, the 'Hanuman' reference was removed in India). Lord Hanuman is one of the most popular Gods in India. He is simple, large-hearted and a powerful warrior. *Black Panther*'s reference to Lord Hanuman is not mere fiction. He was once worshipped by warriors across many parts of the ancient world. Indeed, the ships sailing on the trade rounds on the Indian Ocean rim (between eastern Africa, Arabia, Persia, India and Southeast Asia) carried not only goods and cloth, but philosophies and tales of Indian Gods and Goddesses. In return, African ideas, materials and people arrived on the shores of India. The Siddhis (originally from ancient Ethiopia and Kenya) came to India many centuries ago and rose to become great traders, generals and even kings and queens over time. Many of them converted to Hinduism or Islam. They adopted Indian ways. Today they speak Indian languages such as Marathi and Gujarati.

But India and Africa share another, darker commonality: they have both been victims of rapacious invaders. India, just like Africa, suffered substantially in the past few centuries. Angus Maddison, a British economic historian, stated that India was the No. 1 economy in the world in the centuries before the British arrived. Regrettably, by the time the Turkic and European invaders were done with us, we were a byword for poverty and backwardness. Ancient India had yielded a tremendous crop of knowledge, not just in the domain of spirituality but also in mathematics, metallurgy, astronomy, medicine, navigation, water management, textiles, etc. India had among the oldest universities in the world. Many aspects of India's culture were destroyed by invaders; most famously, Nalanda University. It was the largest university of its time, with more than 10,000 students. It was burnt to cinders in 1193 by Turkic invader Bakhtiyar Khilji.

Historians estimate that man-made famines killed thirty million to thirty-five million Indians during the British Raj. The Bengal Famine of 1943–44, to name but one, was the result of conscious war policies of Winston Churchill. An estimated four million Indians starved to death because of his decisions. When local Raj officials messaged him about the devastation, the great 'war hero' purportedly wondered why Gandhi was still alive.

Indians could be like Killmonger (played by Michael B. Jordan) and react to past crimes with hatred, anger and vengeance. Or one can be like T'Challa (Chadwick Boseman), who acknowledged historical crimes but without anger and hatred. Instead of seeking revenge, he instead worked to make Wakanda strong. My mother, a very wise woman, once said to me, if you hate someone more than you love yourself, there is no hope for you.

Watching *Black Panther* is also a reminder of the regrettable strains in the modern India–Africa relationship. Indians remember the mass expulsion from Uganda under Idi Amin in the 1970s. Africans feel the racism of modern India toward them. There have been reports of attacks on African students in India. But these go against the grain of traditional African–Indian ties. Even in the recent past, India inspired decolonization movements across Africa. India has invested in varied fields such as energy and telecommunications in Africa. Ghana's Presidential Palace was built with Indian aid. I couldn't help but notice that many of the traditional clothes in *Black Panther* had a mix of African and Indian designs.

Africa and India would do well to remember the ways of their ancestors, approach each other with liberalism and respect, and build a new future.

The other forceful message emerging from *Black Panther* is the importance of pride. Wakanda may be fictional, but the ancient Songhai and Great Zimbabwe kingdoms are not. They have been airbrushed from history. Africans would do well to revive the memories of these great empires, which will fill them with pride and confidence and can be the fuel for greatness. India and Africa must remember the great achievements of our ancestors, infuse ourselves with pride and strive toward scaling greater heights today—and not because we want to prove something to the invaders and colonialists who once brought us to our knees. We must make grand achievements today so that we can prove ourselves worthy descendants of our remarkable ancestors.

'Wakanda Forever!' is the salute in the film. But if you'll permit me, I'll also say 'Africa Forever!' and 'India Forever!' too.

First published in *The Washington Post*, 12 March 2018

India's Increasing Influence

'There is more power in blue jeans and rock and roll than the entire Red Army.'

—Régis Debray, French leftist philosopher and former comrade-in-arms of Che Guevara

Régis Debray could be accused of hyperbole in his conception of the attractiveness of Western popular culture and soft power. But his statement cannot be accused of having no substance. He said this in 1986. Prescient, considering the events that followed by the end of that decade.

Theories in international relations are very clear on this subject. A country's ability to meet its objectives is constrained by the extent of power it wields. And it must be accepted that there is no substitute for hard power; any serious country must wield it. But soft power works as a force-multiplier, making the use of hard power that much more efficient.

This is a fair argument.

But do we confuse causality at times? Can it also be that soft power or culture, can lead to hard power over the long term? Is it possible that a country's culture (the root of soft power) creates the conditions for strengthening its own hard power?

The Flow of Influence

It has been said that politics is upstream of policies, just as culture is upstream of politics.

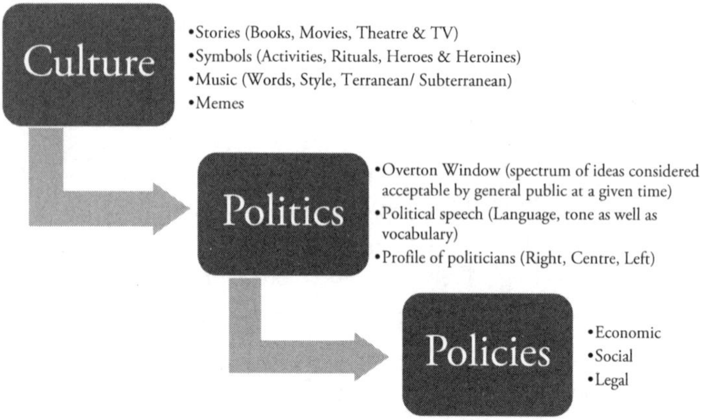

The graphic above is a simple illustration of the idea that the cultural space impacts politics over time. And politics impacts the viability of policies over the following years. The flow is usually upstream to downstream, much like a river. And it is a one-to-many relationship (I will explain this subsequently in the chapter).

So, if one intends to implement policies that strengthen a nation (e.g., investing in a strong army), one must bring in the politics that make this possible (i.e., strong national consciousness). And space for the requisite politics will be created, over a long period, by culture.

Any effort to change major policies, without having created the political ground for it, is difficult and risky. For example, implementing reformist economic policies in Europe during the financial crisis had prematurely ended many promising political careers. Luxembourg politician Jean-Claude Juncker had once pithily remarked on reforms, 'We all know what to do, we just don't know how to get re-elected after we've done it!' Even in India, many economic reforms have been brought in by stealth. Our savvy politicians are aware that economic reforms alone rarely win you the elections. Only when economic reforms are linked to appropriate political issues, will they be accepted. For example, GST implementation was linked with the politically resonant call to remove black money and stem corruption. When politics is not ready for certain policies, even if they are in the long-term interest of people, they will be difficult to implement, e.g., the farm reforms in India.

When we follow a natural flow—impact culture first, then politics, and finally policies—it can be surprisingly easy to ring in change; even transformation. Merely fifteen to twenty years ago, it would have been inconceivable to think that laws could be changed to recognize LGBT marriages in the West. Remember, added to widespread prejudice against LGBTs was also the fact that homosexual relations had been stigmatized by the affliction of AIDS. But the ground was created culturally when LGBT relations found acceptance by a new generation. The prolific presence of gays and lesbians in cultural powerhouse communities (like Hollywood, Western TV, Western social media companies), drove mass acceptance and comfort. Once the cultural ground was created, politics began to change. The way even a liberal President like Bill Clinton spoke carefully of LGBT rights in his public comments, as compared to how a conservative-supported President Trump spoke supportively without any hesitation a mere decade-and-a-half later, signalled the huge political shift that had occurred. Once politics was aligned, changing laws was a matter of time. Furthermore, the cultural power of the West enabled liberalizing of LGBT laws across the world, including in India. It must be stated that India's ancient culture did not criminalize LGBT relations. This made the task easier here.

So, to sum up, if politics is the Ganga and Sundarbans the policies at the end of the great river, then Gangotri is culture.

The Many-to-one Relationship between Culture, Politics and Policies

A key concept in this relationship from upstream to downstream is the impact of one-to-many. It is not a one-to-one relationship. Let me elucidate this point: *one* cultural meme group can have a disproportionate impact on *many* political processes. And *each* political process in turn can have an impact on *multiple* policy options.

So just one powerful cultural meme group (e.g., proponents of LGBT rights) can impact thousands of policies across the world.

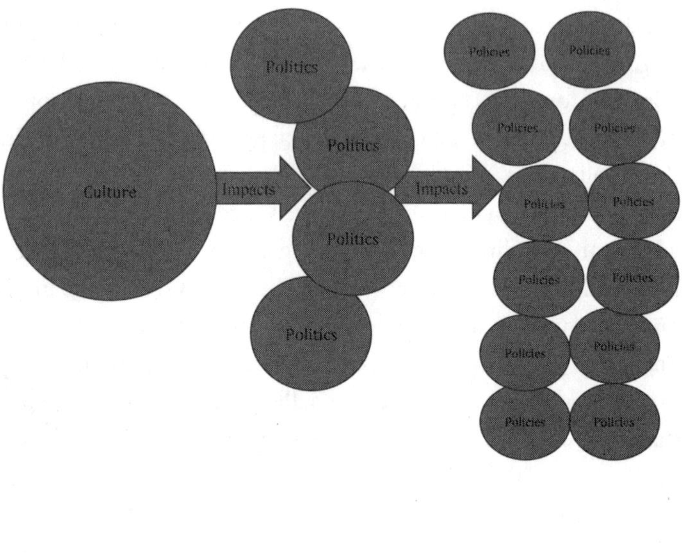

Coming to India ... *Ramayan* and *Mahabharat* were relayed on television—Doordarshan—in the mid-1980s to early 1990s; as also Chanakya, *Bharat Ek Khoj* [Discovery of India], *Hum Log, Buniyaad* and a few other teleserials. These TV serials had a huge impact on the culture of India. Over the next few decades, this cultural phenomenon (besides some other factors) had a transformational impact on politics. And now, the political impact is playing out in policies. Think about it: less than ten TV programmes relayed over thirty years ago are impacting policies today that affect 1.3 billion people on this planet. The impact of one-to-many.

Any work in the area of culture is a huge force-multiplier over time.

So Where Will Indian Soft Power Be in the Post-Covid-19 World?

But First, Where Are We Today?

Largely, in popular Western culture, we have been ignored post-Independence. This is especially true in the most powerful Anglophone (English-speaking world) culture. The *Global Soft Power Index Report* is among the world's most comprehensive research studies on perceptions of soft power. In its 2020 report, India ranked a low twenty-seven, behind even relatively tiny economies like Finland and Ireland. And it is particularly disheartening to learn that this too was an improvement on previous research findings. India simply does not have a profile worthy of a country that is the fifth largest economy in the world and accommodates one-fifth of humanity (a nation that has more people than North America, Europe and the Middle East combined). Our economic under-performance in the pre-1991 era had an adverse impact overall, notwithstanding a brief period of some visibility when a few mainstream Western music bands in the 1960s and 1970s discovered Indian spirituality and yoga. The most impactful among them were The Beatles (driven largely by the huge interest George Harrison had in India and Indian culture). As a result, yoga and Indian spirituality took off in the flower-power fraternity among the baby-boomers of the West. That involvement with yoga filtered into the mainstream a few years later as its benefits seeped into Western consciousness; albeit largely the physical components, less so the spiritual aspects. The popularity of His Holiness the Dalai Lama, and the resultant interest in Buddhism, also fanned this nascent involvement with the Indian ethos. Fortunately, and very positively, over the recent years, India has built on this pre-existing interest in yoga around the world and taken symbolic ownership of this physical, mental and spiritual practice. The Government of India sponsored the recognition of the International Day of Yoga at the UN and with this one inspired act, added dramatically to our soft power. The increasing popularity of many new-age Indian gurus across the world has also helped. Mahatma Gandhi is ubiquitously well-known across mainstream Western culture, and the impact of Richard Attenborough's film (released in 1982) cannot be denied in adding to this aura.

In recent years in some circles, particularly the Indology departments of academia and sections of mainstream Western media, our image has turned negative. We are viewed as an uppity third-world country that has forgotten its place; case in point, the calls by senior white journalists to block the minuscule Western aid to India in response to India's neutrality during the Ukraine crisis or the racist cartoon from *The New York Times* upon the successful Indian Mars Mission. But while these academic and media attacks on India may upset opinion-makers in our country, these opinions are niche and not well-known in the mainstream of Western countries. Social media is prone to exaggerate the strength of these bombasts.

The real narrative problem about India is that our visibility in popular Western culture and mainstream Western academia/media is relatively low, given our heft as the second most populous nation and economic stature as the fifth-largest economy in the world.

One cannot have a positive (or even a negative) image, if one has no image.

Reality Driving Soft Power

This has begun to change slowly over the last few years. The augmented visibility of Indian government programmes has indeed increased our visibility. The unprecedented success of the International Day of Yoga deserves a special mention in this regard. Our growing economic heft will add to this virtuous cycle, as more and more people across the world experience an Indian product or service. The Indian diaspora is a very powerful asset, both to the mother culture of India and to the countries they have made their home. Indians are called the 'model minority' in the West, with their superlative economic and academic achievements. In the recent past, the Indian community has also started garnering political power in their adopted nations; two of the top four members of the present Cabinet in the UK are of Indian origin.

Our IT and scientific prowess, based on recent performance in the IT industry and achievements like our *Mangalyaan* and satellite launches, have had a laddering impact and created an impression of high Indian intellect in the Western mind. The intellectual geek Indian is becoming an occasional presence in the Western entertainment industry: contrast Rajesh Koothrappali in the hit mainstream American TV series *The Big Bang Theory* (2007 onwards) with the almost complete absence of an Indian character in *Friends* (1994 onwards); or even the inane character Apu in *The Simpsons* (1987 onwards). Rajesh essayed one of the main characters in the *The Big Bang Theory* ensemble, although it is still quite rare to find a mainstream lead Indian character in Western popular culture; though one does find more than a few programmes with Chinese lead characters.

The turmoil across the world since the Covid-19 pandemic began, has further enhanced the image of the strength of the Indian system. It was assumed that India would not be able to vaccinate its huge population rapidly enough, keeping in mind the glacial speed at which our polio vaccination had rolled out (from the 1990s) when compared to the rest of the world. But India not only invented and manufactured its own vaccines (which have among the highest efficacy rates), it has also administered nearly 1.8 billion doses with over 800 million Indians fully vaccinated. India has not suffered the political divisions that have bedevilled many other countries in the world, in terms of unscientific opposition to vaccination and roll-out of other measures to control the spread of Covid-19. The death rate in India per million due to Covid-19 is far lower than in the developed countries of the West. Also, unlike many Western nations—which let vaccine stocks within their countries go waste rather than help the rest of the world—India has exported a huge number of vaccines to poorer nations, in its spirit of *vasudhaiva kutumbakam* (the world is one family).

India has successfully conducted some of the largest evacuation programmes across the world from war zones like from Yemen in 2015 (*Operation Raahat*) and Ukraine in 2022 (*Operation Ganga*). We helped people of other nationalities as well, even Pakistanis. The world also noticed that when a powerful northern neighbour attacked us, unlike some other countries that crumbled when they were thus tested, India stood its ground and fought back. Our infrastructure is improving by leaps and bounds. Our capabilities in high-quality manufacturing and services are grabbing attention across the world.

All this is impacting our image. Capability and confident conduct create their own soft power. And vastly improved Indian capabilities will lead to stronger soft power over this decade.

But, as has been argued in the early part of this chapter, causality can move the other way as well. Culture (or let us say, the building blocks of soft power) can also generate hard power.

Culture Driving Reality and Hence Hard Power

While India has been building capabilities—and we have had many cultural revival projects in India (e.g., the Kashi Vishwanath Dham Project)—we have not focused as much on building our soft power attractiveness globally. This lacuna must be corrected. We must engage with cultural influencers across the world and get our message across; and keep in mind that in the cultural space, the Hyper Pareto Principle holds ground: 1 per cent of the influencers have more impact than 99 per cent of the others.

How do we ensure that our country's narrative and messaging is covered in movies, books, documentaries, mainstream media and social media channels, besides others that influence the world? The best cultural minds in the country must work on this.

And this will also have a real economic impact. For instance, the tourism industry. Across the world this critical industry generates large-scale employment, allowing prosperity and development to reach the far corners of a nation. Remember, infrastructure and law and order must improve to ensure tourist influx, besides supporting the survival and spread of the nation's culture. This industry must make rapid progress in India. Even more, foreign tourists carry back memories of Indian culture, and can become potential ambassadors of our soft power. In recent years our infrastructure has improved tremendously, and the end of the pandemic will revive the travel industry, but we must also address our image among the elites of the tourism industry. The perception that India is unsafe for women is not without some substance and India must improve its law and order to set this right. But countries with far worse security for women, such as some in Europe, do not have as odious a reputation. While even a single woman being harassed is one too many, data clearly shows that casting India as one of the most unsafe places in the world for women is not supported by numbers. India is actually among the mid-level countries in the world as far as safety for women is concerned; far better than even some countries in western Europe. However, Western media narratives have created an impression different from data among the tourism industry elites. The real data must be communicated and projected to outsiders.

The tourism industry is one among many sectors in which India's position and image, among the Western and non-Western elites, is misrepresented, contrary to India's reality; Kashmir, the Russia–Ukraine War, and the recent farmer protests, are other cases in point. Powerful countries have independent cultural spokespersons who explain the country's position, even while being critical on occasion. We must engage with those who are interested in India, rather than ignore them if they are not 'cheerleaders'.

A World Pagan Festival is an idea whose time has come, and India must lead this celebration of the ancient past. Let us make it a regular feature in India. The Indic way of life is the last surviving major Pagan way of life (even Southeast Asia, China and Japan have historically been deeply influenced by our culture). We are the only pre-Bronze-Age culture that is still alive and breathing. In ancient times India's cultural influence had spread to many countries to our west as well, for example, Mittanis in the Middle East and Mithraism in ancient Rome. Most other ancient Pagan ways of life have been destroyed. But there is a revival of modern interest in Paganism (which includes idol worship, Goddess-worship, nature-worship and atheism among others) across the world, especially in the West. Of note is the popularity of OTT teleserials like *Outlander* and *Vikings*. India can be a natural leader of this movement—we can support the revival of Paganism globally with this festival. It would place us in the central arena of soft power across the world. Our ancient heritage and knowledge, including that of yoga, the epics, astrology, dance and music, fit naturally into this strategy. We could, for instance, combine this with our *Kumbh Mela* events.

We should institute the Indian equivalents of the Eisenhower and Fulbright fellowships. Under their aegis, we should invite American and Chinese (and many other nationalities too) mid-career, emerging leaders in the cultural and academic space, to India on a Fellowship programme and give them a deeper insight into India and access to leadership across the fields of politics, business, culture and administration. These fellows will, over time, build their careers with a deeper understanding of India and work as brand ambassadors for our nation.

Generation and dissemination of knowledge can be another vital source of soft power. For example, it has been tabulated by the National Mission for Manuscripts that there are over three million handwritten Sanskrit manuscripts (as compared to between 20,000 to 30,000 handwritten Greek manuscripts) that survive to this day. Our ancestors have bequeathed us an ocean of knowledge, which is as yet an undiscovered treasure. This knowledge extends from spirituality to astronomy, mathematics, physics, chemistry, medicine, metallurgy and many other streams. As part of our soft power project, we should invite and fund Indian and India-sympathetic scholars from around the world to translate and share this knowledge with the world, provided that correct attribution is given to India in their works. This can dramatically raise India's soft power profile as a centre for knowledge, a *Vishwa Guru*. The National Mission for Manuscripts can be a very strong partner in this endeavour.

Lastly, keeping in mind that many soft power tools (such as Western social media companies and mainstream media outfits) have been weaponized over the recent past, we must refocus Indian minds for *atmanirbharta* in not just the hard power sectors like military and finance, but also in soft power and culture. We need indigenous social media companies and cultural influencers, our own mainstream media companies and data control so that we engage with developed nations as equals.

Conclusion

This chapter merely provides some preliminary thoughts and direction. It is safe to say that India is rapidly changing in a positive direction, and this pace will increase in the next couple of decades. The next two decades will see more change than has been seen in the last few centuries. This is an exciting time to be an Indian. There is a lot to be done in the cultural space. Let's get down to it!

First published in *Modi: Shaping a Global Order in Flux*, February 2023

Indian Soft Power

Both established theory and received wisdom seem to agree that soft power propagation tends to follow hard power conquest. Greco-Roman culture enveloped most of Europe on the heels of Roman legionaries. The Arab conquest of the Middle East and North Africa preceded the dominance of the Arabic language, culture and way of life across the region. The cultural dominance of the Anglosphere across the modern world is a remnant of the humongous power exercised by the British empire, which was built on warfare. However, hard power does not necessarily lead to soft power. Mongols established one of the largest empires in human history, yet the soft power of Mongolia, from the Mongolian language to the Tengri religion to native Mongolian culture is hardly visible outside Mongolia.

It would seem a safe conclusion, then, that soft power is most often built on the back of hard power conquest. And equally, that hard power is not a guarantee for soft power to automatically emerge. Hard power appears to be a 'necessary but not sufficient' condition for soft power.

Is there any model in history that breaks this rule? Did a culture do the impossible, i.e., spread its soft power through much of the known world without necessarily resorting to any hard power projection abroad?

Yes, there is such a model actually; of a country whose soft power spread across more than half the global population at the time, for more than a millennium (from the first century CE to around the twelfth century CE), without almost any overseas military conquest. A country whose way of life, religions, philosophies, stories, rituals, music, and sometimes even names, were absorbed and accepted by millions of people in foreign lands. A country that succeeded in casting many others in its own image (to varying extents), without apparently trying to. A country that did not use the imposition of *force*; it instead used the pull of *attraction*. A country that sent traders, scholars, storytellers, scientists, priests, mathematicians, sculptors, painters, musicians, metallurgists and many others to foreign lands, but rarely sent an invading army. A land that was called *Bharatvarsha* in those days; today, in its much-shrunken state, we know it as India.

It's a remarkable story. It should be studied in a serious manner. It hasn't been. Not even by the modern descendants of those great men and women of ancient Bharatvarsha. More on the lack of confidence among modern Indians later.

Remnants of that soft power triumph of Bharatvarsha (which comprised the entire Indian subcontinent), in the first millennium CE, are visible to this day. The clearest examples are available in Southeast Asia where locals adopted Sanskritized names, built Indian-style temples, reorganized their societies in keeping with Indian theories, had Indian-style rituals, and worshipped Hindu Gods and Goddesses (with their own regional variations). In East and Central Asia, Buddhism was absorbed into the daily warp and weft of life. While it merged into the local traditions of Japanese Shintoism and Chinese Confucianism, in Central Asia on the other hand, Buddhism (with a mix of Hinduism) formed almost the entire basis of life. Ruins of temples with Sanskrit inscriptions dot the landscape of central Asian towns to this day. The lingering impact of this can be seen in languages too. Over 20 per cent of the Tocharian (modern north-western China) vocabulary is from Sanskrit. The Scythians of Central Asia used the ancient Indian Brahmi script to write their own language. Brahmi inscriptions of Sanskrit have been found in Kara Tepe, Uzbekistan. Pre-nineteenth-century Japanese world maps usually depicted India as the centre of the World.

South Asia, Southeast Asia, East Asia and Central Asia accounted for over half the global population at the time.

Indian influence was widespread, massive, and so strong that elements of it survive to this day in these far-flung regions, long after the decline of India, owing to repeated conquests by foreign invaders in the second millennium CE (from the eleventh century onwards). Thereafter, large parts of the Indian subcontinent were ruled almost continuously by outsiders: first the Turkic invaders and then European colonialists, till its independence in the mid-twentieth century.

Constrained by both maximum word count, as well as lack of serious study of this remarkable phenomenon, I'd like to quickly propose some theories on why Indian soft power spread far and wide in the first millennium, despite almost no hard power projection abroad (besides the brief conquest of Southeast Asia by Indian emperor Rajendra Chola in the eleventh century). They could serve as lessons, not just for Indians today, but for others as well.

1) Domestic Strength

The heart of global soft power lies in domestic strength. A nation must be genuinely successful to be worthy of emulation by other countries. If it lacks confidence, is riven with infighting, or is being beaten on the world stage by others, it doesn't either inspire or attract. This started happening to India by the beginning of the second millennium CE, and as its domestic strength waned, its soft power abroad emaciated as well. This is happening to some Western powers today.

2) Economic Success

According to British Economic historian Angus Maddison, India accounted for approximately 30 per cent of global GDP through the first millennium CE. It was, by far, the richest land on earth at the time. This was of course based on India's massive population (which some historians suggest was a result of better medical and hygiene standards, relative to the rest of the world at the time). India, like many other countries in the world, was a largely agrarian economy during that period. But trade played a huge role as well. Historian Sanjeev Sanyal has written about the tremendous importance of the Indian Ocean trade routes, as compared to the more fabled land-based Silk Route. Ships have much greater carrying capacity than camels/oxen. Also, the Indian Ocean is unique in that the winds change direction, every year, like clockwork, because of the monsoon system. This made a round-trip, annual trade route possible. In the early first millennium CE, Roman historian Pliny rued Roman addiction to Indian goods and the massive trade deficit, resulting in the outflow of Roman gold to India. With the invasions of the second millennium CE, and some superstitions seeping into Indian culture about overseas travel, trading declined relatively. Agriculture suffered as well under the onslaught and disruption caused by foreign marauders. India slowly lost its wealth dominance, and hence, became less influential. Western powers must ponder on this as their global trading confidence and domestic production reduces.

3) Liberal and Open-minded Spirit

India is home to one of the oldest Jewish communities in the world, who sought refuge in the first/second century CE after their temple in Jerusalem was destroyed by the Romans. Zoroastrian Persians found a home in India when they fled Arab oppression in the seventh century. We imported some royal dynasties as well on occasion (when the reigning dynasty did not have legal heirs). Women occupied a very high status in ancient India when compared to most other ancient cultures. LGBTQ lifestyles were not criminalized. The founder of one of the greatest Indian ruling dynasties, the Chandravanshis (Lord Krishna was a Chandravanshi), was a transgender called Ila. We were a practical and pragmatic people, which meant that we were liberal because it was the smart thing to do, not because we were 'virtue-signalling' our moral superiority. And we benefitted from it.

4) Knowledge and Science

As foreign travellers have recorded, ancient Indians were most obsessed with knowledge. We hosted the oldest and greatest universities in the ancient world: Nalanda, Takshashila, and

Sharada Peeth, to name just a few. Students flocked to these universities from all over the planet. Numerous schools and temples across the subcontinent met the need for primary schooling and feeding of the poor. There were great innovations in sciences, mathematics, metallurgy, navigation and agriculture among other areas. Much of it was documented as well. Despite the massive destruction of almost all ancient Indian universities in the invasions of the second millennium CE, at least three million hand-written Sanskrit (India's ancient language) manuscripts survive to this day, according to the National Manuscript Mission. This is more than that of the rest of the ancient world combined. The modern West credits knowledge of algorithms to the Arab scholar Al-Khwarizmi. But Al-Khwarizmi himself was clear about the source of large portions of his knowledge; he named his book *Kitab al hisab al Hindi* (Book of Hindu Numerals/Maths). The modern West credits Fibonacci (a.k.a Leonardo Bonacci) with the Fibonacci series, but Fibonacci himself, in his book, *Liber Abaci*, called it the 'Indian Series'. Having said that, from the thirteenth to fourteenth century onwards, it is difficult to recall any new epoch-making knowledge innovation that Indians came up with. We simply stopped being productive in the field of knowledge, outside of a few regions like Kerala, where the Kerala School of Mathematics flourished in the sixteenth century. As our knowledge production declined, our soft power declined.

5) Warrior Spirit

Today, India is largely viewed as a fundamentally pacifist and non-violent culture. But this is often a backward projection of Mahatma Gandhi's aura into ancient history. Yes, India indeed has ancient pacifist and non-violent traditions. It is also true that rarely did Indians march out of the Indian subcontinent to conquer foreign lands. But it is equally true that Indians did not lack warrior spirit, and there is documented evidence of massive wars between Indian kingdoms and empires. It is also true that till the beginning of the second millennium CE, India regularly beat back foreign invaders. The Huns destroyed much of ancient Europe but were repeatedly pushed back from India. 'Alexander the Great' could not make much of an entry into the subcontinent, and he didn't even battle the heartland Indian empire of the time; he was fended off by the relatively smaller kingdoms at the borders. So, India did possess hard power. But it was always defensive hard power, never offensive. Military strength was used to defend the motherland, but rarely to conquer foreign lands. This ensured that we protected that which was precious. And by not focusing on conquering foreign lands, Indians skirted a classical reason for the downfall of great powers: overreach. However, from the twelfth century onwards, as our defensive hard power declined, many foreign invaders succeeded in conquering India. Those invasions ripped through the heart of medieval India. Thousands of temples were destroyed, tens of universities were burnt to the ground, millions were killed, knowledge was lost, and much of the Indian subcontinent became a defeated, conquered land. Noted American historian Will Durant had said the invasion of India was perhaps the bloodiest in human history. Soft power was the least of what we lost. We lost much else and have just about survived. If a nation cannot protect itself, it's only a matter of time before invaders will rob it of its treasures. What was the reason for these military defeats faced repeatedly by India? Too much infighting? Excess pacifism? Outdated military technologies? Rigid overconfidence and disdain even as emerging powers we looked down upon challenged us? Catastrophic success with its inevitable pitfalls? Combination of all? Perhaps.

India fell so drastically over the last 800 years, that many modern Indians are shocked when they travel abroad and see remnants of our ancient culture represented in foreign lands. For we have forgotten too much. Modern Indians need to understand the reasons for the success of our ancestors and try to revive that spirit. And perhaps, modern Western powers can also learn from how ancient India lost its mojo and attempt to not repeat those mistakes. The story of ancient India has many lessons for the modern world, in as much as it has lessons for modern Indians on what they can be again.

First published in 'Global Soft Power Index Report', 2020
(by Brand Finance UK)

It's All about Balance

As the Coronavirus pandemic spreads across the world, I am in London, where the death counts have been troubling and worrying. If any event can be called a global black swan event in our collective lifetimes, this pandemic is it. Of course, some debate that it is not the disease itself that is a black swan, but the global reaction to it. That though, is a subject for another day, one that can be debated more fully a year or two later, when the total fatalities of this disease are finally clear.

But one thing that is already clear, is that it is a time of enormous transformations at several levels, whether ecological, national, societal or individual.

Let's start with the definition of a virus. It's an organism that multiplies at an uncontrollable pace and is so acquisitive that it destroys the very thing that gives it sustenance. In many ways, that is probably how Mother Earth must see humanity. The extended lockdown across the globe has allowed the planet to breathe again, its skies are bluer, its rivers are cleaner, and its animals are not feeling cornered. It may be a bad time for humanity, but it's a good time for the environment. Can humanity learn something from this? A sense of balance in what we desire, perhaps? So that we don't behave like a virus infecting Mother Earth?

At a national level, governments across the world, authoritarian or democratic, are tracking citizens at an unprecedented level. Most people will accept this with the fair belief that there is no choice; it has to be done for everyone to be safe and healthy. Will this level of surveillance continue once the pandemic is over?

At the societal level, there will be two distinct directions. Either societies will rediscover their traditions, and spirituality, and find strength in each other. There is already a questioning of the excess individualism of the last few decades which has resulted in increasing loneliness across much of the world. Or societies will embrace even greater individualism, echoing in some ways the Roaring Twenties, where hedonism, drugs and self-indulgence were a reaction to the twin tragedies of the Spanish Flu and the First World War. I think India will rediscover traditions and spirituality. Where the West will go, is still open to question.

At the individual level too, there will be a change, a move away from the economic model of the last century which had consumerism at its core. Its upside was the huge growth in economies, which allowed so many things we take for granted today; an enormous number of people being pulled out of poverty and a standard of living for middle classes befitting the royals of little over a century ago. But its downside was the devastation of nature and growing unhappiness despite the material wealth. Will humanity find a balance between materialism and spirituality? One hopes so.

How will things play out for India? I feel that this pandemic, and its consequences, will do to India as a whole what Y2K did to our IT industry: a paradigm shift. It's easy to forget how Indians were seen before the Y2K projects across the world. There was the usual bigoted imagery of snake charmers and elephants. But post Y2K, Indians came to be seen as brainy and reliable, and India quickly became a back-office to the world.

I think the way we have managed this pandemic till now (and there is reason to believe we will continue in this vein) will cause another paradigm shift. Our governments have moved decisively. People have been reasonably disciplined about the quarantine; let's be honest, with our limited state capacity, if too many people had refused to follow the lockdown, there was little the state could have done. Our politicians have simply requested, and most people have followed. It's a remarkable quality in us that we Indians can be chaotic in normal times, but extraordinarily disciplined and focused in times of crisis. Many societies are exactly the opposite. And the results clearly show in our numbers; not just the Covid-19 deaths, but even overall deaths due to unnatural causes have come down.

There are many things we can do better, of course. And those criticisms must be made and listened to. But a large part of winning a long war is morale. And our morale should be high considering that we have done reasonably well till now. I believe the extraordinary way Indians have managed themselves in lockdown at a mere request from the leadership comes from a deep attachment to our land. Our self-image may be that of the weak and meek, but, in fact, we are incredibly tough and gritty. This resilience, this steel in the spine, is evident in the way we have negotiated this crisis. Don't forget we are among the very few ancient cultures that still survive despite so many invasions and attacks.

We will emerge stronger on the other side of this crisis. I believe that.

—As told to Kaveree Bamzai

First published in *Open* magazine, May 2020

The Dharma of Skywalkers

The make-believe world of films is compelling. And a well-written one can often be insightful. One such movie series is Star Wars: a meditative anthology on the nature of good and evil. There is much in Episodes IV, V and VI that explores philosophical truisms we can learn from.

The original release of the first Star Wars movie introduced us to a gallery of timeless characters: Yoda, Obi-Wan, Han Solo, Luke and Leia. And of course, Darth Vader. The dramatic joust between good and evil in the storyline fuelled my fascination towards the franchise. And the scene that completely blew my mind; the iconic moment when Darth Vader tells Luke Skywalker, 'No, I am your father!' I was captivated because the intricate plots resonated with much that I had learnt about the ancient dharmic ways at home. Like, when the Jedi are searching for the Chosen One, the intention is not for good to defeat evil. Instead, it is to bring balance to the Force. This is a deeply dharmic thought; a prominent philosophical strain expressed in Hinduism, Jainism, Buddhism and Sikhism. *Ati sarvatra varjayet*, excess or extremes should be avoided, always. For divinity lies in the lap of balance. I hesitated to voice these musings to people outside of my family. They would wonder, I convinced myself, how I was seeing similarities between the philosophies in one of the most successful Hollywood film series of modern times, and ancient Hindu thought.

This is why I was intrigued when I came across an article a few years ago; it was titled, 'The 3,000-year-old sacred story that inspired Star Wars'. It was written by Damien Walter. In a very gentle, well-articulated manner, Walter dwelt on a gripping story set 'a long time ago, in a galaxy far far away', with technical razzmatazz that could wow one to a mush, but one that actually had a deeply ancient and dharmic core.

As J.J. Abrams, the director of *The Force Awakens* is quoted in the article, 'Star Wars was never about science fiction—it was a spiritual story.'

Damien Walter proposes that one of the inspirations for Star Wars was our very own Ramayan, through the masterly work of Joseph Campbell. The choices made by the characters, the nuances in all situations, and our fascination with them, make us learn.

But I think it goes deeper than just the story. Doesn't the Force seem a bit like our Brahman? I must clarify, by Brahman, I do not refer to the caste-group Brahmin. Brahman is the Divine that animates and is at the heart of the entire universe. Much like the Force. Those who truly understand Brahman are the realized souls in the dharmic way. They 'have the force with them'!

In George Lucas' imagined universe, did the Force ultimately find balance? As it turns out, the destruction of the Sith does not lead to balance. For as our ancient Texts say, true balance, the point at which we attain moksha or nirvana is beyond good and evil. And since balance is not restored, even when the Sith die out, a new Dark Side emerges within a generation. It would seem that balance is always an active pursuit, never a passive attainment! More interesting is the fact that the Sith and the Jedi were former brothers in the Force, and it was a schism between the dark and the light side of the Force that drove them apart. Many Indians have forgotten that even the Indian tradition's Asuras (so-called 'demons') and Devas were actually half-siblings and had the same father: Saptrishi Kashyap. Intriguing parallels, wouldn't you say?

In the Indian way, time is circular; not linear with a beginning and an end. And if time is circular, when your journey moves forward, you sometimes realize that you have been here before. But what you enjoy is the journey itself, not the destination. Now let's see where *The Rise of Skywalker* takes this journey of a modern story with an ancient soul.

May the force, and Brahman, be with you!

First published in *India Today*, December 2019

The Misery of the Pandemic and Lessons on Dharma

The two of us usually talk on Sundays—a London–Mumbai conversation. Of late the conversation, back and forth, has been over a book we have worked on. Last Sunday we veered from the pandemic towards authors and worldviews—specifically, two: JRR Tolkien and George RR Martin, the modern era's two highpoints of fantasy fiction literature in the West. The Lord of the Rings and A Song of Ice and Fire (more famous by its TV series name, *Game of Thrones*). Two great authors. Two good men (by most accounts). Two great visions. Two different worldviews.

Some may ask, why turn to Western authors for an insight on dharma? Why not? Goddess Saraswati showers her blessings on all, and wisdom pours in from all corners, unconstrained by human borders of nations and civilizations.

So, the Tolkien worldview is driven by nobility, goodness, clarity of morals, of right and wrong. Even the violence in LOTR is driven by honour. The Martin worldview is dark. Pensive. Brutal. Unforgiving. It is decadent, debauched and violent. GOT often contains no-purpose violence, just because the character can. It is violence from a dark place.

At its heart, LOTR is driven by nobility and virtue, but simplistic judgementalism while GOT is driven by powerplay, absence of morals, but realistic pragmatism.

Tolkien was born in 1892 and died in 1973. He saw it all, for they were brutal decades. First World War: twenty-two million dead. Spanish flu: fifty million dead. Great Depression: unemployment, famine, inflation, ruination. Nazi ascension. Second World War: sixty million dead. Amazingly, humanity survived.

Martin was born in 1948. And the Western world took off from the late 1940s into a Long Peace. He was a baby boomer and grew up in a milieu of well-being in his society. He has seen perhaps the best time ever for humanity, when per capita violence is the lowest ever. Per capita prosperity is the highest ever. Baby boomers had a good life and Martin didn't live through the horrors of a war. He even dodged the faraway Vietnam War.

You'd think their life experiences would define their worldview. Someone who's lived through wars and deprivation would create a dark universe and one who has lived in peace and had the good life would create a sunshine world of light and goodness.

But it's the other way around. Why? How?

Is it that those who suffer, learn? Grow moral? Deepen their nobility (for there is potential nobility in everyone)? Ancient Indians talked about the role of suffering in spiritual growth. Challenges are opportunities. Tough times are a churn and can bestow nobility. Grief can bring out the best in us. Ironically, an easy life can create a sense of drift and descent.

The elite Western youth of today are the most privileged generation in human history. It is difficult to understand why they are so angry. Why the nihilistic and destructive urge, despite having the best life, in material terms, that any generation has ever had?

The Buddha gave us the *Chatvari Arya Satyani, the four noble truths.* A more accurate translation would be four truths for the noble.

The first truth of nobility is *dukha. Grief. Misery.* Life is misery, Buddha said. His concept of dukha was broader than mere suffering. It encompassed a sense of unease and dissatisfaction. The second is *samudaya*, which defines the cause of misery. It is a craving, a cloud of attachments and desires that surround our waking moments. It is a non-positive, unconscious emotional and mental state. The third is *nirodha*, the possibility of ending misery. And the fourth, *marga*, is the path to ending misery.

Misery leads to the Path.

The Covid-19 pandemic, which emerged in Wuhan (China), has taken the world by a psychological storm. There has been death, destruction and economic chaos. Businesses have been wiped out. Over 1.5 million people have died globally. Too many more have suffered and are still suffering. It is terrible, heartbreaking, and an end seems far away. Furthermore, most experts agree that the economic and psychological scars will remain for years, if not decades, even when the pandemic ends.

And so, using the principles of dharma, and the role of grief, will we emerge stronger and wiser from this pandemic? Will we emerge better? Or have many among us, especially the elite, not suffered enough? After all, yes, we have been confined to our homes. Captive, but with running water and food; even innovative recipes. There is the face mask and social distancing, but also electricity, Wi-Fi, Netflix and Amazon Prime.

Have we suffered enough? Do we really need to suffer enough? How much is enough? Can we learn the lesson of the times without the tightest of slaps by Lady Destiny? What would dharma say? Is there a spiritual purpose to the pandemic? Can this be a spiritual opportunity?

It is up to us. Every single one of us.

The lessons abound. We can re-ignite a sense of community. Root ourselves in the cocoon of family, friends, and neighbourhood—meaningful human relationships, rather than the noise of social media. Can we live a life that is larger than our selfish interests, goals and ambitions? The pandemic has taught us that we can live with less. Much less. We have learnt that desires can be both infinite and very finite. It is a mental arrangement. Can we do quiet charity and abandon the egoistic urge to showcase it with press releases and social media posts? We might then open the space for dharma to enter our lives.

We have seen our fellow creatures of other species on this planet heave a sigh of relief. Can we create a better world not just for ourselves but for the animals? For water bodies, mountains and grasslands? For all living species?

Dive within. Divine the message of the times. Reclaim a sense of wonder. And an adult responsibility for all life.

Grief can lead to spiritual growth. Gautam Buddha said so. We should listen.

Written with Bhavna Roy; first published in The Print, December 2020

The True Source of Terror

This article was triggered by an interesting conversation with a correspondent for a Western newspaper, recently. He spoke of Hindu terror in India, which had risen, apparently, in retaliation to Islamic terror. And of course, there was a pious concern for our 'fragile republic'.

Let's leave the pious concern aside. India is a strong country. We're not going to break up. But this constant trope of Hindu terror, and Indian Islamic terror, needs the sunlight of data. Fortunately, data is available. A global terrorism database is maintained by the US-based National Consortium for the Study of Terrorism and Responses to Terrorism. And in this global database, there is detailed information on terror attacks in India as well. This database extends all the way back to 1974 from the present. Some ten thousand unique terrorist incidents have been recorded there. It has been analysed by Rupa Subramanya, whose work I am quoting in this article. There is another database, the South Asian Terrorism Portal, which lists 20,000 terrorist attacks. Their definition of terrorism is broader. The analysis of both these databases is enlightening. The numbers make the story very clear.

Firstly, the so-called Hindu terror charge is utter nonsense. Of the 10,000 terrorist attacks in India, only 0.6 per cent can be classified as 'Hindu terror'. Considering that Hindus make up nearly 80 per cent of India's population, I think it can be safely concluded that there is no problem of Hindu terror in India.

Now let me address what most opinion-makers speak of: Islamic terror in India. Many people, both right-wing and left-wing, allege that radical Islam is the biggest cause of terror in India. But what does the data say? Well, if you remove terrorism in Kashmir, Islamic terrorism makes up just a little over 3 per cent of terrorist incidents in India. That's it. 3 per cent. While I do admit that there is a radical Islamic element in Kashmir (the Kashmiris carried out the only ethnic cleansing in independent India; that of Kashmiri Pandits), it cannot be denied that there is also a geography-based independence element to terrorism in Kashmir. Furthermore, while there is a higher probability of Islamic than Hindu terror acts in India, we must acknowledge that a large part of what is called Islamic terror is actually planned and executed by the Pakistani export-oriented terror industry. Admittedly, the Pakistanis find a few collaborators in India, but policemen I have spoken to acknowledge that many of these terrorists are caught due to the support of the Indian Muslim community. This is patriotism. I do strongly hold that we can only stop Pakistani terrorism when we have moral, intellectual and ethical clarity on the ghastly nature of the Pakistani state; and are not lost in delusional hopes of peace with them. But I will debate with anyone who tries to tar Indian Muslims with the same brush. Indian Muslims are, in the vast majority, as patriotic, peace-loving and inclusive as their Indian Hindu brethren.

So, what is the biggest source of terrorism in India? To the knowledgeable, it will not be a surprise that leftist terror is by far the biggest of them all. You can call the ideological grounding of this terrorism by many names: Marxism, communism, Maoism. But the fact is that 30 per cent of terrorist incidents in India, in the last forty years, were the result of this ideology. In fact, in the last decade, the proportion of leftist terror in all terrorist incidents has gone up to nearly 50 per cent. If we *do* want to reduce terrorism in India, then there needs to be a calm, rational analysis of Marxism/communism/Maoism in the marketplace of ideas. What is it in this ideology that seems to encourage violence? French historian and scholar Stéphane Courtois, in his *The Black Book of Communism*, documented that over ninety million people died under communist regimes across the world in the last hundred years; through man-made famines, mass murders, ethnic cleansing, etc. Even in India, anecdotal evidence suggests that political violence seems to be highest where the ideology of communism/Marxism is strong: in West Bengal and Kerala. I am not suggesting that we collectively blame all communists and Marxists personally; for they too are victims and prisoners of this ideology. But I think the ideology needs careful calm analysis, and perhaps reformation. Communism/Marxism needs to explicitly give up violence and hatred for the other.

Differences are fine. There is no way that all of us can have the same point of view. And we are India. We celebrate different points of view. We celebrate questioning everyone, including God. Vedic Sanskrit had no translation for the English word blasphemy.

But using violence to settle differences with other Indians is not okay. That is obvious.

First published in *DNA*, April 2017

Time to Understand the CAA, with Reason

Emotions cloud the mind and hijack reason. They're powerful. It's futile to attempt debate without addressing emotions. For they must subside for the mind to work. Around the Citizenship Amendment Act (CAA), heightened emotions are ripping asunder social compacts. I was heartbroken by the cruel words used by some Hindus on the great cricketer Irfan Pathan's Twitter timeline. *Irfan jaise watan ke wafaadaar pe shaq karna adharma hai*. Equally, as an idol-worshipper, I was outraged by some of the sloganeering at Jamia Milia Islamia such as 'All idols will be removed and only Allah's name will remain.' These words may belong to Pakistani poet Faiz, but to hear them in India, which has suffered horrific iconoclastic violence by barbaric fanatics such as Mahmud Ghazni, Sikandar Butshikan and Aurangzeb, is cruel. These heightened emotions have led to heartrending violence. We must calm down; we are all children of Mother India. Every other identity we carry is of lesser consequence than this.

Calming down will also open space for reasoned debate on this amendment to our Citizenship Act. It must be understood that all it does is open an accelerated path to citizenship for minorities from Pakistan, Bangladesh and Afghanistan, who've already sought refuge in India before December 2014. This does NOT close the door on the Muslim majority in these three republics. They can seek refuge in India as per the existing standard process. Individuals such as Adnan Sami have applied for and received Indian citizenship. In 2015, India granted citizenship to nearly 15,000 Bangladeshis, mostly Muslims. So why was this amendment necessary for the minorities (Hindus, Christians, Sikhs, Buddhists, Jains and Parsees) of the three Muslim-majority republics of the subcontinent? Because they face extinction-level persecution. It's the same principle on which refuge was given to Jews during the Nazi era or Yezidis during Islamic State rule in Syria.

Countries that offered this refuge were not perfect in their treatment of minorities. The US gave refuge to many Yezidis, but their treatment of African-Americans is a work-in-process. Also, these countries did not 'establish fairness' by offering a similar accelerated path to citizenship to everyone from beleaguered Syria.

So what was the principle here? That all minority rights, like equality, protecting language/culture, etc., are built on a very fundamental right: right to life. If minorities are wiped out, through mass murder, forced conversions, and expulsions, all other rights become redundant. Has the right to life of the minorities in Pakistan been attacked, and has extreme oppression been a long-term state pogrom, rather than short-term politics of a particular regime (in which the external world could interfere and help)? Base your judgement on data. Minorities are disappearing fast in these three subcontinental Muslim-majority republics. According to the Pakistani scholar Farahnaz Ispahani, around 1947, minorities comprised 23 per cent of the West and

East Pakistan population. This has now fallen to 3 per cent in Pakistan (former West Pakistan), and a little over 9 per cent in Bangladesh (former East Pakistan). The greatest fall occurred in 1971, when three million Bangladeshis, mostly Hindus, were massacred by the Pakistani army. Extrapolate the reduced percentage of minorities to the present population, and there are over sixty million missing Hindus, Christians, Sikhs and other minorities in Pakistan, Bangladesh and Afghanistan.

In 1950, Prime Minister Nehru signed the Nehru–Liaquat pact with Pakistan Prime Minister Liaquat Ali Khan, in which India promised to look after its Muslim minority and Pakistan, its non-Muslim minority. India has honoured its half of the pact. During this period the population proportion of Muslims in India has increased from under 10 per cent to over 14 per cent. But in Pakistan and Bangladesh, perhaps one of the biggest ethnic cleansings of the past century has occurred with sixty million fewer minorities than there should have been.

This amendment is attempting to protect six besieged minorities from extinction. It does not prevent individual refugees from the Muslim communities of Pakistan, Bangladesh and Afghanistan from continuing to come to India through the normal process, which many Afghan Muslims have already done. And it certainly does not affect any Indian citizen, Muslims included. All claims to the contrary are false.

To criticize India for this amendment would be akin to criticizing those countries that specifically took in Jews in the mid-twentieth century to save them from extinction, by claiming it would be an anti-Christian act.

Surprisingly, none are questioning the Muslim-majority republics in the subcontinent for the sixty million missing minorities. Bangladesh and Afghanistan are at least working at protecting their remaining minorities now. But Pakistan … well what can one say…

Lies travel halfway around the world before Truth can even get its shoes on. Misinformation around this amendment has claimed lives. Property has been destroyed indiscriminately. This is appalling. According to the Joint Committee of the Indian Parliament, only a little over 30,000 Hindus (mostly backward-castes and Dalits), Christians, Sikhs, Buddhists, Jains and Parsees will immediately benefit from this amendment, and that too after rigorous vetting from Indian security agencies. And I repeat, India gave citizenship to nearly 15,000 Bangladeshis in 2015, most of them Muslim. Now what would you say to those who say that India is losing its secular ways, while at the same time ignoring the burning issue of sixty million missing minorities in the three Muslim-majority republics of the Indian subcontinent?

Truth must be told. With calmness. But it must be told.

First published in *Hindustan Times*, December 2019

Other Titles by Amish

The Shiva Trilogy

The fastest-selling book series in the history of Indian publishing

THE IMMORTALS OF MELUHA

(Book 1 of the Trilogy)

1900 BC. What modern Indians mistakenly call the Indus Valley Civilization, the inhabitants of that period knew as the land of Meluha – a near perfect empire created many centuries earlier by Lord Ram. Now their primary river Saraswati is drying, and they face terrorist attacks from their enemies from the east. Will their prophesied hero, the Neelkanth, emerge to destroy evil?

THE SECRET OF THE NAGAS

(Book 2 of the Trilogy)

The sinister Naga warrior has killed his friend Brahaspati and now stalks his wife, Sati. Shiva, who is the prophesied destroyer of evil, will not rest till he finds his demonic adversary. His thirst for revenge will lead him to the door of the Nagas, the serpent people. Fierce battles will be fought and unbelievable secrets revealed in the second part of the Shiva trilogy.

THE OATH OF THE VAYUPUTRAS

(Book 3 of the Trilogy)

Shiva reaches the Naga capital, Panchavati, and prepares for a holy war against his true enemy. The Neelkanth must not fail, no matter what the cost. In his desperation, he reaches out to the Vayuputras. Will he succeed? And what will be the real cost of battling Evil? Read the concluding part of this bestselling series to find out.

The Ram Chandra Series

The second-fastest-selling book series in the history of Indian publishing

RAM – SCION OF IKSHVAKU

(Book 1 of the Series)

He loves his country and he stands alone for the law. His band of brothers, his wife, Sita, and the fight against the darkness of chaos. He is Prince Ram. Will he rise above the taint that others heap on him? Will his love for Sita sustain him through his struggle? Will he defeat the demon Raavan who destroyed his childhood? Will he fulfil the destiny of the Vishnu? Begin an epic journey with Amish's latest: the Ram Chandra Series.

SITA – WARRIOR OF MITHILA

(Book 2 of the Series)

An abandoned baby is found in a field. She is adopted by the ruler of Mithila, a powerless kingdom, ignored by all. Nobody believes this child will amount to much. But they are wrong. For she is no ordinary girl. She is Sita. Through an innovative multi-linear narrative, Amish takes you deeper into the epic world of the Ram Chandra Series.

RAAVAN – ENEMY OF ARYAVARTA

(Book 3 of the Series)

Raavan is determined to be a giant among men, to conquer, plunder, and seize the greatness that he thinks is his right. He is a man of contrasts, of brutal violence and scholarly knowledge. A man who will love without reward and kill without remorse. In this, the third book in the Ram Chandra series, Amish sheds light on Raavan, the king of Lanka. Is he the greatest villain in history or just a man in a dark place, all the time?

WAR OF LANKA

(Book 4 of the Series)

As Raavan kidnaps Sita, Ram seethes with rage and grief. The war of Lanka is imminent; it's a war for Dharma, after all. Will Ram defeat the ruthless and seemingly invincible Raavan? Or will Lanka fight back like a cornered tiger? And, most importantly, will the real Vishnu rise? In this fourth book of the Ram Chandra Series, the narrative strands of Ram, Sita and Raavan crash into each other and explode in a slaughterous war.

Indic Chronicles

LEGEND OF SUHELDEV

Repeated attacks by Mahmud of Ghazni have weakened India's northern regions. Then the Turks raid and destroy one of the holiest temples in the land: the magnificent Lord Shiva temple at Somnath. At this most desperate of times, a warrior rises to defend the nation. King Suheldev—fierce rebel, charismatic leader, inclusive patriot. Read this epic adventure of courage and heroism that recounts the story of that lionhearted warrior and the magnificent Battle of Bahraich.

Non-fiction

DHARMA – DECODING THE EPICS FOR A MEANINGFUL LIFE

In this genre-bending book, the first of a series, Amish and Bhavna dive into the priceless treasure trove of the ancient Indian epics, as well as the vast and complex universe of Amish's Meluha, to explore some of the key concepts of Indian philosophy. Within this book are answers to our many philosophical questions, offered through simple and wise interpretations of our favourite stories.

IDOLS – UNEARTHING THE POWER OF MURTI PUJA

A companion volume to the bestselling *Dharma*, this book brings back your favorite fictional characters, along with some new ones, to explore the essence and true meaning of murti puja. In this insightful book, Amish and Bhavna tackle burning questions about idol worship through simple, varied, and astute interpretations of myths and religious texts. In the process, they reveal the expansive philosophy behind the practice and how it can lead us to experience the Oneness of God through transformation, acceptance, and love.